AF600039

FOUNDED MASSES

according to

THE CODE OF CANON LAW

A DISSERTATION

Submitted to the Faculty of Canon Law of the Catholic University of America in partial fulfillment of the requirements for the Degree of Doctor of Canon Law

by the

REV. NEWTON THOMAS MILLER, J. C. L.

of the Archdiocese of Philadelphia

WASHINGTON, D. C.

1926

Nihil Obstat:

✠ THOMAS J. SHAHAN, S. T. D.,

Censor Deputatus.

Washingtonii, D. C., die XXIX Maii, 1926.

Imprimatur:

✠ D. CARD. DOUGHERTY,

Archiepiscopus Philadelphiensis.

Philadelphiae, die XXIX Maii, 1926.

CONTENTS

INTRODUCTION.

Legislation on founded Masses is important because of the ill repute brought upon the Church by failure to fulfill these obligations. The law safeguards the good name of religion by regulating the acceptance and administration of foundations for Masses as experience has proven necessary. That religion must suffer if such rules are not known, is no uncertain statement. The assumption of obligations that endure for a long time demands prudent foresight lest changing circumstances of time and monetary values later render these obligations unreasonable.

Pastors busied with a multitude of parochial duties, are not infrequently at a loss for time to study the law in detail unless it be presented for their facile consideration. Nevertheless, they may be called upon to administer founded Masses. This work endeavors to supply their need of a short volume in which is gathered the law on founded Masses. The fact that these obligations are practically unknown in the United States enhances the value of this work when need for information does arise.

Authority over the acceptance and administration of foundations for Masses is granted by canons 1545 to 1549, to the local Ordinary. These laws, however, must be applied to founded Masses in churches of religious according to canon 1550 which defines the respective rights and duties of the local Ordinary and the Major Religious Superior. In this dissertation, the plan of the Code has been followed. The term "local Ordinary" has been used unrestrictedly to signify the superior over founded Masses, except in Chapter VIII, according to which one who is concerned with founded Masses in churches of religious should understand the term "local Ordinary" throughout the dissertation.

CHAPTER I.

The Nature of Founded Masses.

In the earliest days of the Christian era, the faithful offered for use in the Holy Sacrifice of the Mass, bread and wine which, after being changed by consecration into the body and blood of Our Lord Jesus Christ, was distributed in Holy Communion. In the course of time, instead of bread and wine, money came to be offered for the sustenance of the priest who offered the divine Sacrifice.

So arose the custom of stipends, long approved by the Church.

From the very inception of this custom, not only were stipends presented to priests for individual Masses but gifts of land and other valuable goods were made to the Church that Masses might be offered for the donors perpetually or for a considerable time.

Such gifts are known as foundations for Masses and the Code of Canon Law states that "temporal goods conveyed to some ecclesiastical juridical (moral) person with the perpetual or long-continued obligation to say Masses, or to perform certain ecclesiastical functions or works of piety or charity in consideration of the revenues received from said foundation," are termed pious foundations.[1]

That a foundation in the canonical sense be established, the obligation must be perpetual or for a long time. Just how many years are required by the term

[1] C. 1544, § 1. *Nomine piarum fundationum significantur bona temporalia alicui personae morali in Ecclesia quoquo modo data, cum onere in perpetuum vel in diuturnum tempus ex reditibus annuis aliquas Missas celebrandi, vel alias praefinitas functiones ecclesiasticas explendi, aut nonnulla pietatis et caritatis opera peragendi.;"* Augustine, "A Commentary on Canon Law," VI, 610.

"long time" is not certain. Vermeersch[2] says fifty years, while Blat[3] says forty, basing his conclusion on analogy with a "*diuturna consuetudo.*"

The obligation incurred by accepting such a gift depends upon the will of the donor, expressed either in writing or by word of mouth. He may lawfully specify that the income be used for the performance of ecclesiastical functions or works of piety or charity; in fine, for any purpose that is possible and honest, *i. e.*, not contrary to divine or natural law.[4]

A work of purely natural philanthropy would not suffice.[5] The Church is supernatural in its purpose and the purpose of endowments to her must consequently be supernatural.

The celebration or application of Masses, the recital of prayers, the erection or sustenance of monasteries, seminaries, academies, schools, hospitals, orphanages—any of these may be cared for by the income from an endowment to the Church for that specific purpose. The present subject, however, is limited to Masses to be celebrated because of such an endowment.

Founded Masses are Masses for which the stipends are derived from the income on an endowment given to an ecclesiastical moral person for the perpetual or long-continued celebration of Masses.

The donor of this endowment may be anyone who by natural and ecclesiastical law may freely dispose of his goods.[6] Canon law does not recognize any right of civil law to limit anyone's right to donate goods to the church for pious causes.

---

[2] "*Epitome Iuris Canonici,*" II, 865.
[3] "*Commentarium Textus Codicis Iuris Canonici.*" Lib. III, P. II, 461.
[4] Bargilliat, "*Praelectiones Iuris Canonici,*" II, 1514.
[5] Wernz, "*Jus Decretalium,*" III, 195.
[6] C. 1513, § 1, "*Qui ex iure naturae et ecclesiastico libere valet de suis bonis statuere, potest ad causas pias, sive per actum inter vivos sive per actum mortis causa, bona relinquere.*"

The recipient of the endowment for founded Masses must be an ecclesiastical moral person.[7]

By an ecclesiastical moral person is meant "a juridical entity, formally constituted by public ecclesiastical authority, subsisting, by concession of law, independently of singular persons and invested with the capacity of acquiring and exercising rights in the Church." [8]

The constitution of an ecclesiastical moral person by the proper public ecclesiastical authority is essential.

The constituting authority may be either divine or human. "The Catholic Church and the Apostolic See have the nature of a legal person by Divine ordinance. The other inferior legal persons get their personality either by law (as the College of Cardinals, a Cathedral Chapter,) or by a special concession of the competent ecclesiastical superior through a formal decree, for the purpose of religion or charity," as confraternities, benefices.[9]

The stipend for a founded Mass is derived from the income on the endowment. The income itself does not

---

7 Cfr. c. 1544, § 1.

8 *"Ens juridicum, publica auctoritate formaliter constitutum, independenter a personis singularibus ex iuris concessione subsistens, atque capacitate iuris acquirendi exercendique donatum."* (Maroto, *"Institutiones Iuris Canonici,"* I, 458). In this definition, the phrase *"ex iuris concessione subsistens"* must be understood to embrace the modes of acquiring moral personality specified by canon 100, *i. e.*, *"ex ipsa ordinatione divina: ex ipso iuris praescripto: ex speciali competentis Superioris ecclesiastici concessione data per formale decretum."*

9 C. 100, § 1, *"Catholica Ecclesia et Apostolica Sedes moralis personae rationem habent ex ipsa ordinatione divina; cererae inferiores personae morales in Ecclesia eam sortiumtur sive ex ipso iuris praescripto sive ex speciali competentis Superioris ecclesiastici concessione data per formale decretum ad finem religiosum vel caritativum."* Woywod, "The New Canon Law," 77; Cfr. Ayrinhac, "General Legislation in the New Code of Canon Law," 215.

constitute the stipend, but is rather the source of the stipend.[10]

The source of a founded stipend distinguishes it from manual and "*ad instar manualium*" stipends, as is evident from canon 826.

> "Manual stipends are called those which the faithful offer out of their own devotion, or from some obligation, even a perpetual one imposed on heirs by the testator.
>
> '*Ad instar manualium*' are called the stipends of foundation Masses which cannot be applied in the proper church, or not by those who, according to the laws of those foundation Masses, should say them, and which may either by law or by papal indult be given to other priests to say."[11]

Other stipends, received from the income of foundations, are called founded stipends or founded Masses.[12]

The Code follows the decree "*Ut debita*" in distinguishing manual and "*ad instar manualium*" stipends.[13]

> "*Declarat in primis S. C. manuales Missas praesenti decreto intelligi et haberi eas omnes quas fideles oblata manuali stipe celebrari postulant, cuilibet vel quomodocumque, sive brevi manu, sive in testamentis, hanc stipem tradant, dummodo perpet-*

---

[10] C. 826, § 3, "*Alia stipendia quae ex fundationum reditibus percipiuntur, appellantur fundata seu Missae fundatae.;*" Cfr. Vermeersch, "*Epitome Iuris Canonici,*" II, 104.

[11] Woywod, "The New Canon Law," 669.

[12] C. 826, § 1. "*Stipendia quae a fidelibus pro Missis offeruntur sive ex propria devotione, veluti ad manum, sive ex obligatione etiam perpetua a testatore propriis heredibus facta, manualia dicuntur.*

§ 2. *Ad instar manualium vocantur stipendia Missarum fundatarum, quae applicari non possunt in proprio loco, aut ab iis qui eas applicare deberent secundum tabulas fundationis, et ideo de iure aut Sanctae Sedis indulto aliis sacerdotibus tradendae sunt ut iisdem satisfiat.*

§ 3. *Alia stipendia quae ex fundationum reditibus percipiuntur, appellantur fundata seu Missae fundatae.*"

[13] Ferreres, "*Las Misas Manuales,*" 132.

uam fundationem non constituant, vel talem ac tam diuturnam ut tamquam perpetua haberi debeat. Pariter inter manuales Missas accenseri illas, quae privatae alicujus familiae patrimonium gravant quidem in perpetuum, sed in nulla ecclesia sunt constitutae, quibus Missis ubivis a quibuslibet sacerdotibus, patrisfamilias arbitrio, satisfieri potest. Ad instar manualium vero esse, quae in aliqua ecclesia constitutae, vel beneficiis adnexae, a proprio beneficiario vel in propria ecclesia hac illave de causa applicari non possunt; et ideo aut de jure, aut cum S. Sedis indulto aliis sacerdotibus tradi debent utiisdem satisfiat."[14]

Founded stipends come directly, "*ad instar manualium*" stipends indirectly, *i. e.*, by transfer, from the income of a foundation.

Manual stipends do not come from a foundation either directly or by transfer. They are offered by the faithful of their own devotion or because of an obligation imposed on them as heirs by the testator.

A manual stipend offered by heirs because of an obligation, even perpetual, imposed by the testator, is very similar to a founded stipend. Such a manual stipend, however, is derived from a gift to a physical legal per son, not to a moral ecclesiastical person; consequently the stipend is manual. A gift which supplies founded stipends, must have been given to an ecclesiastical moral person and become Church property.[15]

Del Giudice remarks that the juridical relation is instituted directly between the giver and the celebrant in the case of manual and "*ad instar manualium*" stipends. With founded stipends it is different—this relation exists directly between the foundation and the priest, and

---

[14] S. C. C., decr. "*Ut debita,*" 11 Maii, 1904; Collectanea, 2192.

[15] Cappello, "*De Sacramentis,*" I, 716, 3; Vermeersch, "*Epitome Iuris Canonici,*" II, 865.

only indirectly, *i. e.*, through the foundation, between the priest and the founder.[16]

A foundation, legitimately accepted, has the nature of a bilateral contract: *"do ut facias."* [17]

A pious foundation is not valid without the consent of the competent ecclesiastical authority, for the obligations imposed by a foundation give it the nature of a bilateral contract and no contract is complete without the mutual consent of the giver and the receiver.[18]

The establishment of a pious foundation does not create an ecclesiastical moral person. There is a juridical person already in existence, and this person is obliged by acceptance of the foundation, to perform certain acts in consideration for the goods donated. There is the temporal element on one side and the spiritual on the other, and between both stands the mediator, viz., the moral person. Hence such foundations can be called neither corporations nor institutions.[19]

16 *"Stipendia Missarum,"* Cap. III, 21.

17 C. 1544, § 2. *"Fundatio, legitime acceptata, naturam induit contractus synallagmatici: do ut facias.;"* Woywod, "The New Canon Law," 1338.

18 Wernz, *"Jus Decretalium,"* III, 200.

19 Augustine, "A Commentary on Canon Law," VI, 611.

CHAPTER II.

Origin and Development.

It is impossible to say just when Founded Masses first came into being. Though the faithful established foundations for pious causes from the earliest days of the Church, the precise time when stipends originated is shrouded in uncertainty, and the first appearance of Founded Masses is, as a consequence, equally uncertain. By a founded Mass one means a Mass that fulfills the obligation of a stipend received from the income of an endowment to the Church for that purpose. Such a Mass could not antedate stipends, nor does the fact that history adduces examples of foundations earlier than stipends militate against this contention.

In the ancient formula of donations and oblations which the faithful made to the Church there is found no obligation of Masses. The faithful made the donations absolutely, without any condition, or for the purpose of gaining remembrance in the Sacrifice or in the prayers of ecclesiastics, as the usual expression of the times had it; "*pro remedio animae meae.*" From the fifth to the twelfth century, one finds this phrase continually repeated, and it seems to sound the tenor of the desires of the faithful in return for their offerings. It expressed a request for prayers and the remembrance of their soul at Mass, but not for the particular application of the special fruits of the Sacrifice, after the manner of stipends.[1]

Berlendi holds that the practice of offering stipends existed in some places in the eighth century, and he gives reasons to think that it antedates that time. The custom spread until the twelfth century, when it was practically

[1] Berlendi, "*Delle Obblazioni All' Altare,*" P. II, 1, 3.

universal.[2] Benedict XIV agrees substantially with this position, as does Wernz.[3] Gasparri shows how unsatisfactory he considers the evidence concerning the origin of stipends when he says; "*Quidquid sit de ejus* (*i. e., stipendii*) *origine historica* * * * ."[4]

There is authority for saying that the practice of stipends was a development from the offerings of bread and wine by the faithful on the occasion of the celebration of the Holy Sacrifice. Van Espen says: "The matter of oblations, which at first principally consisted of bread and wine, in later times was changed into money; and so the former custom of offering money at Mass has given way to the modern '*denarius Missarum.*' "[5]

The faithful were at first satisfied with being included in the intention of the celebrant at Mass.[6]

The increase of the flock of Christ until it became an immense multitude, made the daily celebration of many Masses a necessity. The faithful could not make an offering at each of these Masses. As a result, they established the custom of making an offering for which they requested the celebration of Mass for themselves.[7] Gradually money came to be given instead of bread and wine,

---

[2] Berlendi, "*Delle Obblaz. All' Altare,*" P. II, 1, 4.

[3] Benedict XIV, "*De ss. Miss. Sacrif.,*" Lib. III, Cap. 21, lsq; Wernz, "*Jus Decretalium,*" III, 537.

[4] Gasparri, "*De Sanctiss. Euchar.,*" I, 537.

[5] Van Espen, "*de Sim. cir. Benef.,*" Tom. II, p. 1, c. 6, par. 4; Cfr. Berlendi, "*Del. Obblaz.,*" Parte II, 1, 1; Wernz, "*Jus Decretalium,*" III, 537.

[6] "*Primitus Fideles sua munera offerentes non petebant Missam specialiter pro se celebrari, sed sufficere credebant, si Missae Sacrificio devote conjungerentur, atque una cum Sacerdote ipsum Sacrificium offerrent, divinae Misercordiae confidentes sibi applicandum pro ratione Sacrificii et dispositionis.*" (Van Espen, Tom. I, par. 2, tit. 5, "*de Celeb. Mis.,*" c. 5, 11); *Cfr. Berlendi, o.c.,* P. II, 1, 2.

[7] Thomassinus, "*Vetus et Nova Eccl. Disc. cir. Ben.,*" P. III, Lib. I, Cap. LXXII, 1.

since little of this was needed, frequent communion having fallen into desuetude.[8]

A few of the earliest apparent examples of stipends will give a sufficient outline of the earliest stages in their development.

As early as the sixth century one finds an offering not unlike a stipend. S. Remigius, Bishop of Rheims, who died in the year 535, donated a vineyard in his testament, recorded by Floradora, a writer of the tenth century.[9] The purpose of the gift was that the donor's oblation should be offered on the sacred altars every Friday and Sunday. This obligation was for an indefinite time and has some appearance of a foundation for Masses.

In the eighth century, Saint Anselm, Abbot of Nonantola, founded stipends sufficient for the annual celebration in his hospital of three hundred Masses for the living and the dead.[10]

In the ninth century the practice existed of giving "fondi" to the Church, of making oblations for the altar, of assigning stipends to priests for the celebration of a determined number of Masses according to the intention of the donor. Many histories and old documents of that time relate this custom. In 838, the King of England gave donations to a church in order that the priests should celebrate two Masses each week for his intentions. A document of the year 875 records the foundation and endowment of a monastery, stating that no more was asked of the monks than the celebration of

---

8 Binterim, "*Denkwurdigkeiten,*" Vol. 4, part 3, p. 378; Cfr. Keller, "*Mass Stipends,*" Chap. I.

9 "*Vineam, quam Bebrimodus facit, tibi catenus derelinquo, ut diebus sextis et omnibus diebus Dominicis, sacris altaribus mea inde offeratur Oblatio;*" (Berlendi, "*Delle Obblaz.,*" II, 2, 6).

10 "*Ex suis propriis rebus instituit Missas celebrandas pro salute vivorum et mortuorum per singulos annos trecentas;*" (Berlendi, "*Delle Obblaz.,* etc.," Parte II, 3, 1).

three Masses daily in perpetuity for the founders.[11] Note should be made of the perpetuity of this obligation; it certainly has the appearance of a founded Mass.

In the tenth century, the sustenance of priests was no longer derived from the common offerings, but from stipends offered for the Masses which they celebrated. A very definite emolument was assigned for the priest who celebrated daily at a certain altar.[12] This custom of stipends spread gradually until it became universal in the twelfth century.

Church legislation, the guide of customs within the Church, moulded this laudable practice of stipends in accordance with the spirit of her Divine Founder. Foundations, however, furnished matter for ecclesiastical laws long before Founded Masses came into being. Consequently a discussion of legislation on foundations prior to the existence of founded Masses is a logical preface to a study of the law on founded Masses.

After the peace of the Church in the fourth century, houses were erected for the poor and other miserable people.[13] An edict of the Emperor Constantine gave liberty to every one to leave goods to the Catholic Church.[14]

In Justinian Roman Law, provision was made that the pious dispositions of the dead be carried out, and

---

11 Berlendi, *"Delle Obblaz.,"* P. II, 4, 1.

12 *"Ad Altare S. Michaelis dono Mansum meum de Carumbo* (*this was* a fruitful field of a certain measurement), *et vineam . . . et Missas aut ipse, aut suus legatus ante Sacra Altaria quotidie celebret;"* Berlendi, *"Delle Obblaz., etc.,"* Parte II, 5, 6.

13 Wernz, *"Jus Decretalium,"* III, 197.

14 *"Habeat unusquisque licentiam sanctissimo Catholico venerabilique concilio decedens bonorum, quid optaverit, relinquere."* (*Codex Justinianus,* Lib. I, Tit. II, 1).

Bishops were given authority to look after such matters.[15] These two provisions sound the keynote of subsequent legislation on foundations and founded Masses.

One finds in the Decree of Gratian; "*Clerici, qui pauperum dispositioni vel monasteriorum vel martiriorum presunt, sub potestate singularum civitatum episcoporum secundum traditionem canonum perdurent, neque per suam temeritatem episcopi sui moderationem declinent.*"[16]

In the middle ages, when pious foundations increased marvellously, authority was not taken from the Bishop, even though those religious foundations were often united to monasteries.[17] In the Decretals of Gregory IX; "*De enodochiis et aliis similibus locis per sollicitudinem episcoporum, in quorum dioecesi exsistunt, ad easdem utilitates, quibus constituta sunt, ordinentur.*"[18] Clement V ordained; "*. . . . ea, quae ad certum usum largitione sunt destinata fidelium, ad illum debeant, non ad alium, (salva quidem sedis apostolicae auctoritate) converti.*"[19]

The Council of Trent provided that Bishops should execute all pious dispositions; that they should visit all pious places as long as they were not under the immediate protection of the civil rulers.[20] Administrators of

---

[15] "*Sancimus, si quis moriens piam fecerit dispositionem vel per institutionis modum vel per legatum aut fidecommissum aut mortis causa donationem, vel alium quemcumque (modum) legitimum: sive injunxerit pro tempore Episcopo curam agere ut impleantur, quae ipse voluit sive et hoc reticuerit, sive etiam in contrarium prohibuerit: necessitatem habere heredes id quod ordinatum est, facere et adimplere omnino: Quod si id sponte non fecerint, confestim loci Deo amabiles Episcopos, curiosos esse circa haec, et postulare ut illi omnia impleant secundum voluntatem defuncti;*" (Justinian Code, Lib. I, Tit. III, 46).

[16] C. 10, C. XVIII, q. 2.

[17] Thomassinus, "*Vet. et Nov. Eccl. Disc. cir. Ben.,*" P. II, Lib. II, C. 90, n. 1, 5, 6, 10.

[18] Cap. 3, 4, X, de relig. dom., III, 36.

[19] Cap. 2, de relig. com., III, 11, in Clem.

[20] Sess. XXII, de ref. Cap. viii.

pious places were obliged to render account to the Ordinary, unless otherwise provided in the foundation.[21]

The tendency of the parochial movement was derogatory to centralized administration of ecclesiastical goods by the Bishop. Churches originated in the private oratories of landowners and the temporal affairs of these religious centers, the parishes of later date, were often withdrawn as far as possible from episcopal administration. A canon of the Third Council of Toledo, in 589, reenacted subsequently elsewhere, speaks significantly; "There are many who, against the canonical rule, seek to get their own churches consecrated upon such terms as to withdraw their endowment (dotem) from the disposition of the Bishop. This we disapprove in the past and forbid for the future."[22] On the other hand, many ordinances, as that of the Council of Carpentras in 527,[23] make it quite clear that while the Bishop's right was maintained, the practice prevailed of leaving the offerings of the faithful in the church to which they were made, as long as they were needed there. After the landowner built his church, he set himself to find a cleric whom the Bishop might ordain to serve it. The control of the Bishop over such a church lay in the need of the owner to petition from him the consecration of the altar and the ordination of the cleric.[24]

Another aspect of foundations that has occasioned legislation is the conflict between canonical and civil law on the requisites for the validity of testaments in favor of the Church. Alexander III declared that judgment

---

21 Sess. XXII, de ref., Cap. ix.

22 Catholic Encyclopedia, Article, "Property, Ecclesiastical," page 469; Cfr. Chalons, in Mansi, X, 119.

23 Mansi, VIII, 707.

24 Cath. Encycl., Art., "Property, Ecclesiastical."

concerning the force of testaments in favor of the Church should be based upon the canons, not upon civil law.[25]

After indicating the trend of Church law on foundations before the existence of stipends, the next consideration is that of legislation on founded stipends and Masses.

Before the Council of Constance (aa. 1414-1418), the distinction between founded and manual stipends was not apparent in legal terminology; the primary question was that of the legitimacy of stipends. In the Decree of Gratian, one finds texts that hold that they who serve the altar should live by the altar, unless they are culpably deficient in service.[26] At the time of Innocent III, who died in the early part of the thirteenth century, the right of a cleric who served the altar, to live by the altar, no matter how great his personal possessions, became recognized.[27]

In the decrees of the Council of Constance, stipends for Masses became a subject of the discipline of positive

---

25 "*Relatum est auribus nostris, quod quum ad vestrum examen aliqua super testamentis relictis ecclesiae causa deducitur, 'vos secundum humanam, et non divinam legem in ea vultis procedere, et, nisi septem vel quinque idonei testes intervenerint, omnino inde postponitis judicare. Unde quia hujusmodi causae de judiciis ecclesiae, non secundum leges, sed secundum canones debent tractari, et his divina scriptura testante, duo aut tres idonei testes sufficiunt, discretioni vestrae per apostolica scripta Mandamus, quatenus, quum aliqua causa talis ad vestrum fuerit examen deducta, eam non secundum leges, sed secundum decretorum statuta tractetis, et tribus aut duobus legitimis testibus requisitis (situs contenti) quoniam scriptum est: 'In ore duorum vel trium testium stat omne verbum.'*" Cap. 11, X, de test., III, 26.

26 "*Clerici omnes qui ecclesiae fideliter vigilanterque deserviunt, stipendia sanctis laboribus debita secundum servitii sui meritum per ordinationem canonum a sacerdotibus consequentur;*" (c. 10, C. I, q. 2).

27 Del Giudice, "*Stipedenia Missarum,*" Cap. III, 11.

law[28] and from that time they grow in preference to every other laudable custom of alms to a priest on the occasion of his exercise of the power of orders.

Consequent upon the legal recognition of stipends, was the development of institutions or foundations directed towards the repetition of the Sacrifice of the Mass for some determined purpose. The basic ideas of this practice were the applicability of the Sacrifice for the living and the dead, the excellence of this prayer above all other forms of suffrage, and finally the greater fruit that comes from a repetition of the Mass.

After the fifteenth century, the Council of Trent and later theological and canonical doctrine stressed these concepts and impelled the faithful to adopt this means of exerting a pious care for the future. Then arose the distinction between manual and founded stipends and a precision of terminology that had heretofore been lacking. This distinction was due to the advance in popular favor of foundations for Masses and to the juridical forms they assumed.[29]

The principal motive behind canonical legislation for foundations and in particular foundations for Masses, was the necessity that all pious foundations be fulfilled. This principle was explicitly enunciated by the Council of Trent: "*Ratio postulat ut illis quae bene constituta sunt, contrariis ordinationibus non detrahatur. Quando igitur ex beneficiorum quorumcumque erectione seu fundatione, aut aliis constitutionibus, qualitates aliave re-*

[28] Errors of Wicleff, condemned in the Council of Constance; 19. "*Speciales orationes, applicatae uni personae per praelatos vel religiosos, non plus prosunt eidem, quam generale, ceteris paribus.*" 20. "*Confrens eleemosynam Fratribus, est excommunicatus eo facto.*" 25. "*Omnes sunt simoniaci, qui se obligant orare pro aliis, eis in temporalibus subvenientibus;* Mansi, XXVII, 1204, 1208.

[29] Del Giudice, "*Stipendia Missarum,*" Cap. III, 16.

quiruntur, seu certa illis onera sunt injuncta; in beneficiorum collatione, seu in quacumque alia dispositione, eis non derogetur.''[30]

The reluctance of the Holy See to derogate from pious wills of the faithful who establish founded Masses, is evident from its restriction of the faculties for reduction granted in the Council of Trent.[31] The Congregation of the Council was constant in maintaining that these faculties did not extend to Masses established in the foundations of benefices, nor to any Masses except those which had been accepted before the Council of Trent and whose reduction had been made in the first diocesan Synod after that Council.[32]

The zeal of the Holy See for the fulfillment of obligations of Masses, is once again emphasized by a decree of the same Congregation of the Council, promulgated by special authority of Urban VIII.[33] This decree scores those who accept obligations of Masses that they are unable to fulfill. Grave evils and scandal are an inevitable result, deterring the faithful from such works of charity and religion. In order to eradicate such an abuse, the decree commands: 1. That the onera of Masses are to be reduced only by the Holy See; 2. That as many Masses are to be celebrated as there are stipends; 3. That contrary privileges are recalled. Finally, those who have authority to permit the acceptance of foundations for Masses, are instructed lest lack of foresight render fulfillment difficult in the future.

---

30 Sess. XXV, de ref., Cap. 5, Cfr. Sess. XXV, de ref., Cap. 4; "*Sacra Synodus, cupiens haec ad pios usus relicta* (*i. e., Missae celebrandae ex variis defunctorum relictis*), *quo plenius et utilius potest, impleri . . .*"

31 Sess. XXV, de ref., Cap. 4.

32 Benedict XIV, "*De Synodo Dioeces.,*" Lib. XIII, Cap. Ult., XVIII; Pallottini, "*Collectio Omnium,* etc.," Tom. XIV, "Missa," XI, 5.

33 S. C. Concil., decr. "*Cum saepe contingat,*" 21 Junii, 1625; Collectanea, 16.

On the 23rd of December, 1697, the Constitution "Nuper" of Innocent XII[34] resolved doubts concerning the meaning and extent of the above decree of the Congregation of the Council. The Holy See must always be consulted in the reduction of Masses unless the Bishop is expressly conceded reductive power in the foundation —the number of Masses is to be determined according to the will of the founder. If, however, the founder has not stipulated the number, the Ordinary may decide the question.

The purpose of this document is expressed in the following words: "*opportune providere, ut sublatis fraudibus, ac emendata negligentia, piae disponentium seu benefactorum voluntati, fides illibata servetur, defunctorum animabus integra et prompta praestentur suffragia itidemque Deo major gloria et ecclesiis praestantior cultus reddatur.*" Moreover, it is declared that the Holy See condones and reduces Masses only for a very grave reason.

It cannot but be clear that the Holy See has ever been extremely reluctant to reduce Masses. The legislator wishes to have all pious foundations carried out in accordance with the will of the founder and the power of reduction is jealously reserved to the Apostolic See. "It is hardly reasonable to say that among the burdens of Episcopal care, has very recently been placed the great vigilance that is required of them as sacred Pastors, in order that the pious bequests in their dioceses be carried out and the prescribed Masses celebrated in accordance with the will of the founder."[35]

"*Postulat enim, imprimis, jus naturale et divinum: jubent canonicae, civilesque ipsae leges: pluribus denique in locis studiose commendat Sacrosancta Synodus Tridentina, ut voluntates fidelium, facultates suas in pias*

[34] Collectanea, 241.
[35] Benedict XIV, "*De Syn. Dioec.,*" Lib. XIII, Cap. Ult.

causas donantium vel relinquentium, diligentissime impleantur, et in eos precise usus, juxta modum conditionesque iis benevisas, pecunia inde obventa insumatur ad quos destinata fuit, neque in alios convertatur, etsi meliores utilioresque videantur; si secus fieret, fidelium voluntates, quae pro lege habendae sunt, fraudarentur ipsique, magno cum Ecclesiae detrimento, a piis hujusmodi largitionibus retraherentur."[36] Not only positive human law, but the natural and divine law command the diligent fulfilment of the pious wills of the faithful who donate their goods for pious causes. This principle has ever guided the Church, as it guides her now: "*Voluntates fidelium facultates suas in pias causas donantium vel relinquentium, . . . diligentissime impleantur . . .*"[37]

---

36 Instr. S. C. de Prop. Fid., 1807; Collectanea, 689.
37 C. 1514.

CHAPTER III.

CONSTITUTION.

The nature of a foundation for Masses[1] indicates two principles that must guide the reasonable constitution of the conditions of such an obligation. The amount of temporal goods must be sufficient to provide an annual income capable of supplying the demands of the administration of the foundation; this lest the acceptance be foolhardy. Secondly, there must be an equitable distribution of the income; this to facilitate fulfillment.

It is the right of the local Ordinary to prescribe rules concerning the minimum quantity of the dowry for which a foundation for Masses can be admitted, and concerning the equitable distribution of its revenue.[2]

Besides the Roman Pontiff, the term "local Ordinary" includes, each for his own territory, Residential Bishops, Abbots or Prelates "*nullius*" and their Vicars General, Administrators, Vicars and Prefects Apostolic, and those who in case of deficiency of any of these, succeed them in the rule of their territory either by prescription of law or by approved constitutions.[3]

---

[1] C. 1544; "*bona temporalia alicui personae morali in Ecclesia quoquo modo data, cum onere in perpetuum vel in diuturnum tempus ex reditibus annuis aliquas Missas celebrandi. . .*"

[2] C. 1545; "*Loci Ordinarii est normas praescribere de dotis quantitate infra quam pia fundatio admitti nequeat et de ejus fructibus rite distribuendis.*"

[3] C. 198:

"1. *In iure nomine Ordinarii intelliguntur, nisi quis expresse excipiatur, praeter Romanum Pontificem, pro suo quisque territorio Episcopus residentialis, Abbas vel Praelatus nullius eorumque Vicarius Generalis, Administrator, Vicarius et Praefectus Apostolicus, itemque ii qui praedictis deficientibus interim ex iuris praescripto aut ex probatis constitutionibus succedunt in regimine. .*"

"2. *Nomine autem Ordinarii loci seu locorum veniunt omnes recensiti. . .*"

The rules may be general or for a particular foundation, nor does it matter whether they are promulgated in diocesan Synod or outside, since the law does not distinguish nor restrict.

The terms "*dos*" and "*fructus*" signify respectively the "*bona temporalia*" and "*reditus*" of canon 1544.[4]

The amount of the dowry required for any foundation must be decided in view of the resultant obligations. The income must provide not only for the stipends but also for the expenses incidental to administration;[5] the duration of the obligation and the possibility of future diminution of the endowment demand consideration. So arises the question of a diocesan tax for founded Masses.

This canon does not explicitly mention the determination of a founded stipend, but it is implied as a necessary preliminary to the constitution of a minimum endowment. The tax for founded Masses should be greater than the manual stipend since the perpetuity or long duration of the obligation is extrinsic and a just reason for additional remuneration. Moreover, an unforeseen diminution of the endowment is far from impossible and provision should be made for it.[6]

In the constitution of both the manual and founded stipend, it should be remembered that the purpose of a stipend is to care for part of the sustenance of the celebrant. Due to the different circumstances of time and place under which priests live, the amount of the stipend should vary; the established stipend should be changed if living conditions vary so that this seem advisable.

The total sustenance of a priest is not to be supplied by the stipend, for neither the whole day nor a major part of it is required for the celebration of Mass. Be-

---

[4] Blat, "*Commentarium Textus Codicis Iuris Canonici,*" Lib. III, Par. VI, 463; Cfr. Gasparri, "*De Ss. Euch.,*" I, 559.

[5] Cappello, "*De Sac.,*" I, 716, 2.

[6] Gasparri; "*De Ss. Euch.,*" I, 554; Benedict XIV, "*De Syn. Dioec.,*" Lib. V, Cap. VIII, n. 11.

sides, no secular is promoted to sacred orders without provision for his sustenance nor is anyone admitted to religion unless he can be supported by the income of the monastery or customary oblations.[7] On the other hand, the stipend should not be so small that it corresponds only to the time required for the celebration of Mass. This act impedes a priest during a great part of the day from performing other works by which he might earn his sustenance. Moreover, the Bishop should consider the labor, journey, hour, solemnity and perpetuity of the Mass, and even the parochial office. He might constitute a different stipend for the different hours of celebration, the different distances of churches, the varying solemnities of Masses. In this case, a part of the tax would be for the extrinsic and accidental labor.

Avarice has given occasion to abuses concerning stipends[8] and anything that savors of this vice must be sedulously guarded against by the Bishop: " . . . *ordinarii locorum episcopi ea omnia prohibere atque e medio tollere sedulo curent ac teneantur, quae vel avaritia, idolorum servitus, vel irreverentia, quae ab impietate vix sejuncta esse potest, vel superstitio, verae pietatis falsa imitatrix, induxit.*"[9]

Benedict XIV says that obedience to the above command of the Council of Trent demands that Bishops establish a stipend in their dioceses beyond which nothing can be exacted, a prescription found in the Code of Canon Law.[10]

---

[7] Benedict XIV, *"De Syn. Dioec.,"* Lib. V, Cap. IX, n. 1.

[8] Benedict XIV, *"De Ss. Mis. Sacr.,"* Lib. III, Cap. XXI, 9.

[9] Council of Trent; Sess. XXII, *"Decretum de Observandis,* etc."

[10] *"Ut itaque Episcopi Tridentino obtemperent, atque importunas et immoderatas eleemosynarum pro Missis exactiones impediant, debent, in sua quisque dioecesi, Missarum stipem taxare, ultra quam nemo quidquam exigere valeat;"* (*"De Sac. Mis. Sac.,"* Lib. III, Cap. XXI, 10; C. 831, § 1, *"Ordinarii loci est manualem missarum stipem in sua dioecesi definire per decretum, quantum fieri potest, in dioecesana synodo latum."*

When the endowment of a foundation for Masses is smaller than the minimum prescribed by the local Ordinary, is the acceptance of the foundation illicit or also invalid?

Blat says such acceptance is neither licit nor valid.[11] He bases his contention of invalidity on the tenor of the following canon, the invalidating force of which is not established. The following canon requires the consent of the local Ordinary in writing for the acceptance of a foundation by a moral person.[12] A detailed treatment of that canon will be given in the next chapter. Suffice it to say here that Cappello denies the invalidity of a foundation accepted without the legitimate written consent of the competent Ordinary.[13]

On the force of the arguments advanced in the next chapter against the foundation of Blat's opinion given above, the invalidity of the acceptance of a foundation whose endowment is smaller than the prescribed minimum is rejected. The nullity of such an act is not expressly nor equivalently stated.[14]

The will of the founder is the law regarding the distribution of the income unless it conflicts with the rules of the local Ordinary or superior law. If the stipulated conditions are not satisfactory, the moral person

---

11 "*. . . de dotis quantitate . . . infra quam veluti limitem inferiorem pia fundatio quaelibet in genere vel in specie, . . . admitti nequeat nec licite, nec valide ob sequentis canonis tenorem, . . .;*" (*Commentar. Text. Cod. Iur. Can.,*" Lib. III, Pars. VI, 463).

12 C. 1546; "*Ut hujusmodi fundationes a persona morali acceptari possint, requiritur consensus Ordinarii loci, in scriptis datus, . . .*"

13 "*Si fundatio acceptetur sine Ordinarii consensu, estne valida? Est illicita quidem, sed valida, quia ius canonicum clausulam irritantem non continet; neque iure antiquo licentia Ordinarii sub poena nullitatis requirebatur.;*" ("*Tract. Can.—Mor. de Sacr.,*" I, 716, d). Cfr. footnote (6) on page 575 of the above work.

14 C. 11; *Irritantes aut inhabilitantes eae tantum leges habendae sunt, quibus aut actum esse nullum aut inhabilem esse personam expresse vel aequivalenter statuitur.*"

can refuse the foundation, but acceptance cannot be followed by an arbitrary change of the conditions.

What if the founder has failed to determine in detail the distribution of the income? Then the local Ordinary is empowered to determine the allotment of the revenue.

Benedict XIV[15] quotes a decree of the Sacred Congregation of the Council that is relative: "... *Sacra Congregatio Concilii, interrogata: Primo, Quanta debeat esse eleemosyna Missarum manualium, Secundo, Quanta esse debeat pro perpetuis, non taxatis a Fundatore: die* 15 *Novembris*, 1698, *respondit: Ad primum et secundum, censuit, attendendam esse consuetudinem loci, vel legem Synodalem quatenus adsit; sin minus statuendam esse per Episcopum eleemosynam competentem ejus arbitrio.*"

The local Ordinary is evidently empowered to decide the amount of the stipend when the foundation is established directly by testament or by the founder while alive unless this condition is determined by the founder himself.

What of a foundation established by an heir because of an obligation arising from a legacy in which the testator prescribed only the number of Masses. The heir assumes the place of the founder as donor of the endowment. May he decide the amount of the stipend as the founder?

The Constitution "Nuper" resolved this difficulty. The heir has no right to decide the amount of the stipend. This case is under the authority of the local Ordinary,

---

15 *"De Ss. Mis. Sacr.,"* Lib. III, Cap. XXI, 11; ex Lib. 48 decretor. pag. 584.

who should prescribe the stipend in accordance with the customary tax.[16]

Consideration of the fact that the founded stipend is greater than that for manual Masses for reasons extrinsic to the celebration of the Mass, may prove of assistance to the local Ordinary in determining an equitable distribution of the revenue. The application of a founded Mass gives the celebrant title to no greater return than that due a priest who applies a manual Mass under similar circumstances. Moreover, the founder may reasonably be presumed to have intended to benefit the moral person to which he gave the foundation.

---

[16] "*Posito, quod Testator relinquat, ut celebrentur pro eius Anima centum Missae, absque ulla praescriptione eleemosynae. Quaeritur, an liberum sit haeredibus, eleemosynam sibi bene visam praescribere, an vero eadem eleemosyna praescribenda sit ab Ordinario.*

"*Censuit, ubi nullam certam eleemosynam Testator reliquit, esse ab Episcopo praescribendam eleemosynam congruam, quae respondeat oneribus Missarum celebrandarum, secundum morem Civitatis, vel Provinciae.;*" (Innocent XII, Const. "*Nuper,*" 23 dec. 1697; Fontes, n. 260).

CHAPTER IV

ACCEPTANCE.

It has already been stated that a canonical pious foundation can be established only when the endowment is given to and accepted by an ecclesiastical moral person.[1]

A moral person in the Church was defined as "a juridical entity, formally constituted by public authority, subsisting, by concession of law, independently of singular persons, and invested with the capacity of acquiring and exercising rights."[2]

Moral persons in the Church, the existence of which is explicitly stated in the Code,[3] are distinct from physical ecclesiastical persons, *i. e.*, individual men who have been baptized. "Canonical personality or capacity to acquire and exercise rights in the Church, which goes by divine ordinance with individual human nature and the reception of Baptism, may also be conferred by public ecclesiastical authority upon corporate bodies or institutions which thus obtain prerogatives normally reserved to individual rational beings and, for that reason, are called moral or legal, as distinct from physical or individual, persons."[4]

All moral persons in the Church owe their existence to the intervention of the proper public authority. Divine authority has conceded moral personality only to the Catholic Church and the Apostolic See, the latter of which does not include here the Roman Congregations,

---

[1] Cfr. Chapter I.

[2] Maroto, "*Institutiones Iuris Canonici,*" I, 458.

[3] Cfr. c. 99.

[4] Ayrinhac, "General Legislation in the New Code of Canon Law," 213.

Tribunals and Offices; these are excluded *"ex natura rei"* because they have been created by ecclesiastical authority, not directly by God Himself.[5] Other ecclesiastical moral persons are constituted by ecclesiastical authority, either by law itself, as the College of Cardinals, or by a special decree of the competent Superior, who must be discovered in each case from the provisions of the Code concerning the various classes of moral persons.[6]

The following do not suffice for the constitution of a moral ecclesiastical person; a) the fact of consociation or foundation of some pious work although the end in either case be religious or charitable, when the formal decree of erection is lacking, b) the concession of moral personality in civil law by civil authority, for in such a case canon law recognizes the civil legal personality but not the ecclesiastical moral personality, c) simple approbation of ecclesiastical authority, which is required for the constitution of a collective person, such as a pious union.[7]

A collective body is not a moral person, but, as the name implies, a collection of persons who have put together some of their powers and rights. Such a body receives its existence and rights from its members, while a moral person is constituted in the Church by the authority of God, either immediately or through the Church. Hence the legal personality of a moral person is distinct

---

[5] Cfr. c. 7.

[6] C. 100, § 1; *"Catholica Ecclesia et Apostolica Sedes moralis personae rationem habent ex ipsa ordinatione divina; ceterae inferiores personae morales in Ecclesia eam sortiuntur sive ex ipso iuris praescripto sive ex speciali competentis Superioris ecclesiastici concessione data per formale decretum, ad finem religiosum vel caritativum.;"* Ayrinhac, "General Legislation in the New Code of Canon Law," 213.

[7] C. 708; Maroto, *"Instit. Iur.* Can.," 460.

from that of its members and may continue for some time after they have died. This is not true of a collective body.[8]

A moral person, by its very nature perpetual, is extinguished if it is suppressed by legitimate authority or if it has been disorganized for a period of one hundred years.[9]

An ecclesiastical moral person is the legitimate recipient of an endowment for pious works but the authority of the local Ordinary to prescribe rules concerning the minimum dowry for founded Masses and the equitable distribution of the income, is efficiently safeguarded; his consent in writing must be obtained before a moral person is free to accept any foundation.

"Ut hujusmodi fundationes a persona morali acceptari possint, requiritur consensus Ordinarii loci, in scriptis datus, qui eum ne praebeat, antequam legitime compererit personam moralem tum novo oneri suscipiendo, tum antiquis jam susceptis satisfacere posse; maximeque caveat ut reditus omnino respondeant oneribus adjunctis secundum cujusque dioecesis morem."[10]

The Code introduces important changes from the terminology of the old law by the clause *"Ut hujusmodi fundationes a persona morali acceptari possint, requiritur consensus Ordinarii loci, in scriptis datus . . . ."* The decree *"cum saepe contingat"* of the Sacred Congregation of the Council, 21st of June, 1625,[11] was as follows: *"Episcopus vero seu ejus Vicarius, aut Generalis vel Provincialis, ubi de licentia pro perpetuis oneribus fuerint requisiti, in singulis casibus diligenter inquirant de singulis Missarum celebrandarum obligationibus*

---

[8] Ayrinhac, "General Legislation in the New Code of Canon Law," 213.

[9] C. 102.

[10] C. 1546, § 1.

[11] Collectanea, n. 16.

cuique Ecclesiae aut Loco pio incumbentibus." Written consent was not required, nor was there any semblance of an irritating clause.

Neither was there in the Constitution "*Nuper*" of Innocent XII,[12] an irritating clause, though that document required written consent: "*Ad haec Sac. Congregatio quibusvis Capitulis, Collegiis, Societatibus, et Congregationibus, necnon omnibus, et singulis Ecclesiarum, ac Piorum Locorum, tam Saecularium, quam Regularium Superioribus, vel aliis ad quos pertinet, districte prohibet, ne in posterum onera perpetua suscipiant Missarum celebrandarum; Saeculares quidem sine Episcopi, vel ejus Generalis Vicarii; Regulares vero sine Generalis, vel Provincialis consensu, et licentia in scriptis, et gratis concedenda.*"

Gasparri[13] holds that a foundation for Masses was valid under the old law if accepted by an ecclesiastical institute without consent and permission of the Superior because neither Urban VIII nor Innocent XII used an irritating clause in their laws. In favor of this position there is a declaration of the Sacred Congregation of the Council, 16 Jan., 1644.[14]

Pignatelli[15] outlines the arguments of those who held the invalidity of perpetual Masses accepted without written permission of the Superior, only that he may refute them: "*At ego contra censeo, idque ex eo, quod lex canonica prohibens tantummodo aliquid fieri, illud non irritat, nisi expresse vel aequivalenter, si fiat, irritum fore decernat.*"

Foundations for Masses, accepted without the requisite permission of the competent Superior, were valid

---

12. 23 Dec., 1697; Fontes, 260.

13 "*De Ss. Euch.,*" I, 561.

14. "*Atque ita in hac specie declaratum invenio a S. Congregatione Concilii in Romana 16 Januarii, 1644, scilicet acceptationes hujusmodi oneris Missarum sine licentia Superioris non esse nullas, neque invalidas;*" (Pignatelli, "*Consultationes Canonicae,*" Tom. IV, Cons. CCXXII).

15 "*Consult.* Can.," l.c.

before the Code. What of the new law? Has it wrought a change?

Cappello holds the validity of such acceptance under the Code because canon law contains no irritating clause.[16] His conclusion is based on the fact that neither under the old law nor under the Code, does one find an irritating clause in the law. He apparently considers that the phrase "*acceptari possint*" of the Code, is without any semblance of irritating force, but he offers no argument against the position taken by Blat that the acceptance of foundations without written consent of the local Ordinary is invalid.[17]

Blat, however, offers no argument for his opinion, seemingly basing it upon the Code's innovation of the word "*possint.*" That argument seems insufficient; Cappello's conclusion seems to stand. Canon 6 establishes a presumption against departure from the old law and its interpretation by approved authors. One must prove beyond doubt that c. 1546, § 1, is irritating, for irritating and inhabilitating laws do not urge in doubt of law.[18] Has the term "*possint*" sufficient force indubitably to establish the irritating power of this law? In canon 938 § 2,[19] the last word "*possit*" surely does not mean that the sacrament of Extreme Unction is dependent for its validity on license or necessity. Moreover, the

---

16. "*Tract. Can.-Mor. de Sac.,*" I, 716, d; "*Si fundatio acceptetur sine Ordinarii consensu, estne valida? Est illicita quidem, sed valida, quia ius canonicum clausulam irritantem non continet; neque iure antiquo licentia Ordinarii sub poena nullitatis requirebatur.*" Cfr. footnote (6) on page 575 of Cappello, l.c.

17 Blat, "*Comment. Text. Cod.,*" Lib. III, Pars. VI, 464; "*Ut hujusmodi fundationes a persona morali acceptari ad earum existentiam juridicam possint, requiritur praevie consensus Ordinarii loci, non solum verbotenus vel tacitus vel praesumptus aut indeterminatus, sed in scriptis datus ad hanc singularem fundationem. . . .*"

18 C. 15.

19 "*In casu autem necessitatis, vel de licentia saltem rationabiliter praesumpta ejusdem parochi vel Ordinarii loci, alius quilibet sacerdos hoc sacramentum ministrare possit.*"

legislator could easily have had recourse in canon 1546 to an unequivocal clause,[20] if he meant to promulgate an irritating law.

The departure of c. 1546 from the old law is not evident. Consequently, the acceptance of a foundation for Masses seems valid even without the written consent of the local Ordinary.

The local Ordinary, however, is competent to rescind a foundation accepted without his written consent, at least if it should be a grievous burden to fulfill it.[21] Lucidi[22] grants unrestricted power of rescinding to the Ordinary, but Cappello contends for a distinction: "*Rectius videtur ita distinguendum: vel adest causa iusta rescindendi, vel non. Si habetur causa iusta, ex. gr. si ex fundatione detrimentum potius quam utilitas obveniat ecclesiae, aut si ecclesia nequeat satisfacere antiquis oneribus susceptis et novo suscipiendo, certe potest Ordinarius acceptationem rescindere. Si desit, contra, causa iusta, nequit. Hoc sensu intelligi debet resolutio S. C. Ep. et Reg. in Assisien*, 17 *maii* 1861, *qua nituntur patroni sententiae affirmantis.*"[23]

The local Ordinary should not grant his consent for the acceptance of founded Masses until it is legitimately evident that the moral person is capable of satisfying the new obligations without detriment to those already undertaken. His particular care should be that the revenue correspond to the obligations according to diocesan custom.[24]

---

20 C. 1281, § 1; "*nequeunt valide alienari:*" c. 1532, § 4; "*secus licentia irrita est.*"

21 Gasparri, "*Tract. Can. de Ss. Euch.,*" I, 561; "*at integrum est Ordinario fundationem, forte gravosam, rescindere, uti revera S. C. EE. et RR. in Assisien., Super pio rel. et conc.,* 17 *Maii,* 1861, *rescindendam esse reposuit.*"

22 "*De Vis. Sac. Liminum,*" II, Cap. VII, 55; "*At vero integrum est Ordinario acceptationem rescindere.*"

23 Cappello, "*De Sacr.,*" I, 716, d.

24 C. 1546, § 1.

On the 21st of June, 1625, the Sacred Congregation of the Council made the same provisions: "*...nec antea assensum hujusmodi aut licentiam praebeant, quam eis legitime constiterit, illius sacerdotes, tam novo oneri suscipiendo quam antiquis jam susceptis, satisfacere posse, praecipuamque rationem habeant, ut reditus, qui Ecclesiis et Locis piis relinquuntur, omnino respondeant oneribus adjunctis, secundum morem cujusque civitatis vel provinciae, intelligantque, si in re tanti momenti desides aut negligentes fuerint, in novissimo die hujus praetermissi muneris rationem esse reddituros.*"[25]

The first consideration is that the income be proportionate to the specified number of Masses.[26]

The solution of this question will depend upon the amount of the stipend required for founded Masses, which was discussed in the preceding chapter. Unless the income can supply a just stipend for each Mass after the necessary expenses have been defrayed, refusal of permission for the acceptance of a foundation for Masses is the course of wisdom.[27]

In his estimation of the ability of the moral person to carry out the conditions of a foundation for Masses, the Ordinary of the place should not lose sight of Masses enjoined by previous foundations. When celebration of the Masses is requested in a certain church, the number of priests accustomed to celebrate there for a stipend, is not to be ignored.[28]

Measurement of the capability of the moral person and the income regarding a foundation for Masses requires that the number of Masses be determined. If the founder has not stipulated the number, the Ordinary of

---

25 Collectanea, 16.
26 C. 1546, § 1; Cfr. Blat, "*Comment. Tex. Cod.,*" L. III, P. VI, 464.
27 Gasparri, "*De Euch.,*" I, 562.
28 Gasparri, "*De Euch.,*" I, 562.

the place settles it, according to the diocesan tax for perpetual Masses.[29]

The number of Masses requested by the founder must stand if the foundation be accepted with that condition. Before acceptance, however, the local Ordinary should see that the revenue is sufficient to supply at least the diocesan tax for each Mass that is to be celebrated. A lesser stipend should be refused, although if the founder be still alive, an attempt should be made to settle the difficulty according to justice and equity.[30] When the founder is dead, reduction of the number of Masses can be granted only by the Apostolic See unless the founder has expressly given the Ordinary faculties for reduction.[31] For the will of the founder is the law concerning the conditions of a foundation, and since the number of Masses cannot be arranged with him, the foundation must be accepted or rejected with his conditions unless the supreme ecclesiastical authority intervene. From a canonical standpoint, the local Ordinary might obtain a reduction and accept the foundation. Civil authority, however, might not recognize the validity of an ecclesiastical reduction of the conditions of the contract, and the possibility of a civil suit by the heirs for possession of the endowment in case the conditions are not carried out according to the will of the founder, should influence the procedure of the Ordinary.

The discovery of evidence that only the celebration of Mass was intended by the founder, may permit the acceptance of a foundation that would otherwise require reduction or refusal. For in that case a stipend could be accepted for the application of Masses besides that derived from the foundation for their celebration.

---

29 Cappello, "*De Sacr.*," I, 716, d.
30 Gasparri, "*De Euch.*," I, 562.
31 C. 1551; Cappello, "*De Sac.*," I, 716, d.

An evidently paltry stipend might indicate that the founder desired only the celebration of Mass at a certain hour or in a certain place without application for his intention. A desire for Mass on a certain altar or in a revered church may have prompted the gift, but a contention to that effect must be proven against the contrary legal presumption.[32] Consequently, the local Ordinary must be wary of giving his consent on this score. If, however, one should ask that certain Masses be celebrated and applied, others celebrated, without mention of their application, there would be sufficient indication that the application is not required in the latter case.[33] Similar cases have been decided in this manner by the Sacred Congregation of the Council.[34]

The acceptance of a reasonable foundation should not be unnecessarily delayed, for foundations are gifts, and become valid at the moment of acceptance, not before.[35] They can be recalled by the donor until they are accepted and if the donor dies in the meantime, they are void by law.[36]

The patron of the church has no right over the acceptance constitution and administration of a foundation.[37]

The right of patronage is "a (determinate) sum of privileges, which together with certain duties, are given by the (free) grant of the Church, to Catholic founders of a church, chapel, or benefice, or to those who have a cause (*i. e.*, a lawfully recognized title) from them (the founders)."[38]

---

32 C. 825, 4°.
33 Gasparri, *"De Euch.,"* I, 494.
34 Cfr. Benedict XIV, *"De Sac. Mis. Sacr.,"* Lib. III, Cap. IX, 3.
35 Cappello, *"De Sacr.,"* I, 716.
36 Bargilliat, *"Praelectiones Juris Canonici,"* II, 1515.
37 C. 1546, § 2; *"In acceptatione, constitutione et administratione fundationis patronus ecclesiae nullum ius habet."*
38 Godfrey, "The Right of Patronage according to the Code of Canon Law," Chapter II, part I.

The privileges of a patron[39] give him no right, not not even one of vigilance, over the necessary acceptance of a foundation by the church of which he is the patron. Nor has he a right to regulate in any way, the constitution of the conditions. Moreover, the administration of pious foundations is entirely free of any legitimate interference on his part.[40] This last provision precludes any necessary presentation of the priest to celebrate the founded Masses. Unquestionably, the patron has no right to support from the income of the foundation, even though he be inculpably reduced to a state of want according to c. 1455.

An endowment for Masses, validly accepted, becomes ecclesiastical goods[41] but the laws governing the acquisition and administration of Church goods in general must be applied to such endowments according to the specific prescriptions for foundations in canons 1544 to 1551.

A foundation for Masses may be established either "*per actum inter vivos, per actum ultimae voluntatis sive in testamento sive in legato, et etiam viva voce.*"[42] If possible, however, the solemnities of civil law should be observed in last wills in favor of the Church, but in case of their omission, the heirs should be warned to carry out the will of the testator.[43]

It is evident that the omission of civil solemnities does not excuse the heirs from carrying out the pious

---

39 Cfr. c. 1455.

40 Blat, "*Comment. Text. Cod.,*" Lib. III, Pars VI, 464.

41 Cfr. c. 1497, § 1.

42 Cappello, "*De Sacr.,*" I, 715.

43 C. 1513, § 2; "*In ultimis voluntatibus in bonum Ecclesiae serventur, si fieri possit, sollemnitates iuris civilis; hae si omissae fuerint, heredes moneantur ut testatoris voluntatem adimpleant.*"

works willed by the testator. For the heirs are not to be warned in the above fashion except because of an obligation in conscience that the will of the testator be fulfilled regardless of civil requirements for the validity of the last will. The term "*moneantur*" however, signifies that good faith should not be futilely disturbed nor difficulties in the civil forum be provoked.

CHAPTER V.

Investment of the Endowment.

An effective check has been placed upon undue haste in accepting founded Masses in the two preceding chapters. Now arises the question of wise administration of the endowment. Besides the general laws for the administration of all Church goods, Founded Masses require special precautions. The dowry must be invested safely and so that it provide for the expenses entailed in the fulfillment of the long-enduring obligation of Masses.

"*Pecunia et bona mobilia dotationis nomine assignata, statim in loco tuto, ab eodem Ordinario designando, deponantur ad eum finem ut eadem pecunia vel bonorum mobilium pretium custodiantur et quamprimum caute et utiliter secundum prudens eiusdem Ordinarii arbitrium, auditis et iis quorum interest et dioecesano administrationis Consilio, collocentur in commodum eiusdem fundationis cum expressa et individua mentione oneris.*"[1]

What goods are included under the term "*bona mobilia?*"

Temporal goods of the Church—those which serve temporal life—are corporeal if they are perceptible by the senses, as fields, money; incorporeal if they are perceptible, not by the senses, but by the intellect, as rights and obligations.[2]

Corporeal goods are *movable* if they can move themselves or can be moved from place to place by others, as animals, money; *immovable* if they are not subject to

---

1 C. 1547.

2 Cocchi, "*Commentarium in Codicem Iuris Canonici,*" Lib. III, P. VI, 169; Wernz, "*Jus Decretalium,*" III, 134, III.

local motion without substantial change, as a house or a field.[3]

Corporeal goods only, according to c. 1497, 1, are sub-divided into movable and immovable. Are incorporeal goods subject to this same distinction? Wernz[4] says that rights and obligations,—incorporeal goods—are movable or immovable according to the condition of the thing in which they inhere.

An endowment of money or movable goods must be placed immediately in a safe place designated by the local Ordinary.

The Constitution "*Nuper*" had the same prescription: "*pecunia ac bona mobilia Ecclesiis Locis omnibus, tam Saecularibus, quam Regularibus, atque illorum personis, in futurum simpliciter acquirenda cum onere perpetuo Missarum celebrandarum, ab iis, ad quos pertinet, sub poena interdicti ab ingressu Ecclesiae ipso facto incurrenda a die realis acquisitionis, statim deponi debeant penes Aedem Sacram, vel personam fide, et facultatibus idoneam.*"[5]

Determination of a "*locus tutus*" may be helped by consideration of the phrase "*penes Aedem Sacram, vel personam fide, et facultatibus idoneam.*"

The designation of the safe place, however, is explicitly committed to the local Ordinary. No inferior administrator is of himself competent. This is an innovation in the Code, the old law stating only that the deposition was to be made by those to whom it pertained.

Movable goods themselves should not be put away for safekeeping; they should be sold and their price kept in a safe place, for the Code says: "*bonorum mobilium pretium custodiantur.*" This phrase is an implicit command to sell the movable goods and conserve their price.[6]

---

3 Blat, "*Comment. Text. Cod.,*" L. III, P, VI, 407; c. 1497, § 1.

4 "*Jus Decretalium,*" III, 134, III.

5 Innocent XII, Const. "*Nuper,*" 23 dec. 1697; Fontes 260.

6 Blat, "*Comment. Text. Cod.,*" L. III, P. VI, 465.

The proximate purpose of this deposit in a safe place is to safeguard the endowment from loss or theft: "*ad eum finem ut eadem pecunia vel bonorum mobilium pretium custodiantur ...*"

The ultimate purpose is "*ad eum finem ut eadem pecunia vel bonorum mobilium pretium . . . quamprimum caute et utiliter secundum prudens eiusdem Ordinarii arbitrium, auditis et iis quorum interest et dioecesano administrationis Consilio, collocentur in commodum eiusdem fundationis cum expressa et individua mentione oneris.*" Care lest an imprudent investment cause the loss of the dowry is demanded by the term "*caute*": "*utiliter*" indicates that the income must be in accord with the obligations of the foundation.

The local Ordinary is the judge of the caution and usefulness of the investment, but he is required to hear the interested parties, *i. e.*, the founder and the moral person who has assumed the obligation, together with the diocesan administrative council.

The investment must be for the benefit of the foundation; it must be made with express and individual mention in the document of the investment[7] of the obligations for the fulfillment of which the income must be used.

The question now arises concerning restrictions on this investment. The old law commanded that the investment be "*in bonis immobilibus fructiferis.*" When these immovable goods were alienated by apostolic authority, the price was again to be converted into other stable and fruitful goods.[8]

Cappello[9] holds that, contrary to the old law, the money can be converted, in view of canon 1539, § 2, into "*titulos ad latores*" and into other titles equally safe

---

7 Blat, "*Commentarium Textus Codicis Iuris Canonici,*" Lib. III, P. VI, 465.

8 Innocent XII, Const. "*Nuper,*" 23 dec. 1697; Fontes, 260.

9 "*De Sacr.,*" I, 716, 3; Cfr. Blat, "*Comment. Text. Cod.,*" L. III, P. VI, 455.

and fruitful. Stocks and bonds of societies are not excluded from this class, provided that they are really safe and fruitful.

There is a strong foundation for this opinion. Canon 1547 does not repeat the words of the old law "*in bonis immobilibus fructiferis.*" On the contrary, a phrase is introduced whereby the investment is to be made "*caute et utiliter secundum prudens eiusdem Ordinarii arbitrium.*" This phrase, and the silence of the Code regarding investment in immovable fruitful goods, in view of canon 1539, § 2, seems to require no more than a safe and fruitful investment.

CHAPTER VI.

PUBLIC DOCUMENTS OF FOUNDED MASSES.

Foundations, even those made orally, should be consigned to writing.[1]

The conditions and obligations of all foundations, even though accepted orally, must be expressed in a document which should be legally drawn up or signed by a competent notary, so that they merit public faith.[2] This document, however, has no reference to the validity of the foundation, whether for Masses or other purposes.[3] Its end is to establish legal proof of the foundation in the external ecclesiastical forum, not to comply with the solemnities of civil law.

One copy of this document should be safely preserved in the diocesan archive, the other in the archive of the moral person which has accepted the foundation.[4]

Two authentic documents are to be executed, because the term "*tabula*" is always used to designate public written proof of contracts.[5]

The word "*tuto*" in this canon stresses the need for care lest these documents be stolen, lost or destroyed. With them would perish public proof of the foundation, resulting perhaps, in a multitude of doubts concerning the stipulated conditions.

The diocesan archive is closed; no one is allowed to inspect its documents except by permission of the Bishop

---

[1] C. 1548, § 1; "*Fundationes, etiam viva voce factae, scripto consignentur.*"

[2] Blat, "*Comment. Text. Cod.,*" L. III, P. VI, 466; Cfr. c. 3/2, § 3; c. 373, § 1.

[3] Cappello, "*De Sac.,*" I, 715, 2.

[4] C. 1548, § 2; "*Alterum tabularum exemplar in Curiae archivo, alterum in archivo personae moralis, ad quam fundatio spectat, tuto asservetur.*"

[5] Blat, "*Comment. Text. Cod.,*" L. III, P. VI, 466.

or Vicar General and Chancellor.[6] Documents can be removed from this archive only with consent of the Bishop or Vicar General. They are to be returned after three days, unless this time be extended by the Ordinary. Anyone who takes a document from the archive, must leave with the Chancellor, a document signed by his own hand, signifying that he has that particular document.[7]

The archive of the moral person to whom the pious foundation pertains, should have two inventories or catalogues, one of which is kept in that archive and the other in the diocesan archive. Original documents can be removed from this archive by permission, usually for three days, of the competent Superior. A signed receipt for the removed document must be left with him who is in charge of the archive.[8]

Documents in the diocesan or other archive, not "*sub secreto,*" can be inspected by anyone concerned, who has, moreover, a right to a legitimate exemplar to be made at his expense. Those in charge of archives must observe diocesan rules in granting legitimate exemplars, as well as in conceding permission to examine or remove original documents. When they are doubtful concerning these rules, they should consult the Ordinary of the place.[9]

---

[6] C. 377, 1.
[7] C. 378, §§ 1, 2.
[8] C. 383.
[9] C. 384.

CHAPTER VII.

Fulfilment of Founded Masses.

Founded Masses that have been legitimately constituted and accepted, must be fulfilled. An Instruction of the Sacred Congregation for the Propagation of the Faith states the urgent reasons for this principle; "*postulat imprimis ius naturale et divinum, jubent canonicae, civilesque leges, ut voluntatesfidelium facultates suas in pias causas donantium vel relinquentium, diligentissime impleantur.*"[1] Consequently, the Code has commanded those bound by pious foundations to observe the regulations prescribed in order that pious wills of the faithful be fulfilled, for founded Masses are perhaps the most important class of pious causes.

The prescriptions of canons 1514 and 1517, and of canon 1525 having been observed, there should be drawn up in each church a tablet of the obligations incurred from pious foundations, which tablet should be kept by the rector in a safe place.[2]

Canon 1514 orders that the will of the faithful who give or leave their possessions for pious causes, should be most diligently fulfilled even concerning the mode of administering and erecting the goods, unless there has been admitted an invalid clause contrary to the right of the Ordinary as executor of all pious wills.[3]

The Church has constantly insisted upon this prin-

---

1 *Instr. S. C. de Prop. Fid.*, 1807; Collectanea, 689.

2 C. 1549, § 1; "*Servatis praescriptis* can. 1514-1517 *et* c. 1525, *in qualibet ecclesia, onerum ex piis fundationibus incumbentium, tabella conficiatur, quae apud rectorem in loco tuto conservetur.*"

3 "*Voluntates fidelium facultates suas in pias causas donantium vel relinquentium, sive per actum inter vivos, sive per actum mortis causa, diligentissime impleantur etiam circa modum administrationis et erogationis bonorum, salvo praescripto* can. 1515, § 3."

ciple, as in the Decretals of Gregory IX, when the fulfillment of the desires of a woman who had died intestate, expressing her will only verbally, was insisted upon.[4]

Ordinaries are the executors of all pious wills, whether they be expressed by reason of death or among the living.[5]

An executor of a last will is established either by the testator or by law. The law of this last act is the will of the testator, and the executor established by him holds the first place.[6]

Ordinaries, as executors of pious wills, have the right and the duty of watching even by visitation, that pious wills be fulfilled. Other delegated executors are held accountable to this same Ordinary for the right performance of their duty.[7] Any clause in last wills contrary to these executive rights of Ordinaries are held as non-existent.[8]

This canon is founded on the old law, but the office of executor was then committed to Bishops.[9] The new law substitutes the term Ordinaries, which includes others not signed with the Episcopal character, but enjoying Episcopal or quasi-Episcopal jurisdiction.[10]

The Code omits the phrase of the Council of Trent: "*etiam tanquam Sedis Apostolicae delegati, in casibus a jure concessis.*"[11] Ordinaries no longer act as delegates

---

[4] C. 4, X. Indicante, III, 26; "*Cognovimus . . . quod moriens uxor*" "*Redempti unam concham argenteam nudis verbis iussit venundari et suis dari libertis, et scutellam argenteam cuidam monasterio reliquisse: in quibus utrisque voluntatem ejus per omnia volumus adimpleri.*"

[5] C. 1515, § 1; "*Ordinarii omnium piarum voluntatum tam mortis causa quam inter vivos, exsecutores sunt.*"

[6] Cocchi, "*Comment. in Cod.,*" L. III, P. VI, 194.

[7] C. 1515, § 2.

[8] C. 1515, § 3.

[9] Conc. Trid., Sess. XXII, de ref., c. 8.

[10] Cfr. c. 198, § 1.

[11] Conc. Trid., l.c.

and in cases conceded by law but in all cases and by ordinary power, *i. e.*, by virtue of power granted to their office by law.[12]

Any cleric or religious who accepts goods to be used for pious causes, whether by act among the living or by last will, must make known his acceptance of this trust to the Ordinary and indicate all the accepted goods whether movable or immovable, together with his obligations. If the donor or testator expressly forbids this rendition of account to the Ordinary, the cleric or religious ought not to accept the trust.[13]

Only clerics and religious are under this obligation. The acceptance of a gift or legacy for pious causes would oblige a lay person only to account for his fulfillment of the office of executor and to permit visitation of the Ordinary.[14]

The Ordinary is obliged to demand a safe investment of goods accepted in trust for pious uses and to watch over the faithful execution of the pious will in accordance with his office of executor by canon 1515.[15]

Since the gift in trust to a cleric or religious, is not given over to a moral ecclesiastical person, but to a physical, legal person, a pious foundation is not established.

The Ordinary to whom a religious must render the account required by paragraphs one and two of canon 1516, is the Ordinary of the place, if the goods are to be used for churches or pious causes of the place or diocese, or for people having domiciles there. Otherwise, the

---

[12] C. 197, § 1; Blat, "*Comment. Text. Cod.*,' L. III, P. VI, 427.

[13] C. 1516, § 1; "*Clericus vel religiosus qui bona ad pias causas sive per actum inter vivos, sive ex testamento fiduciarie accepit, debet de sua fiducia Ordinarium certiorem reddere, eique omnia istiusmodi bona seu mobilia seu immobilia cum oneribus adiunctis indicare; quod si donator id expresse et omnino prohibuerit, fiduciam ne acceptet.*"

[14] Vermeersch, "*Epit. Iur. Can.*," II, 836, II.

[15] C. 1516, § 2.

proper superior is the Ordinary of the religious.[16] The local Ordinary is the proper Ordinary of all religious except an exempt clerical religious. For the latter, the proper Ordinary is his Major Superior.[17] "Place" includes Vicariates and Prefectures Apostolic, just as "diocese" signifies also abbacies and prelatures "*nullius.*"[18]

For a discussion of the reduction of pious wills in so far as it concerns founded Masses, the reader is referred to the chapter on that subject.

Contrary customs being reprobated, administrators, whether ecclesiastical or lay, of any church even a cathedral, or pious place canonically erected, or confraternity, are held by reason of their office, to render each year to the local Ordinary, an account of their administration.[19]

Customs contrary to the prescriptions of this paragraph are expressly reprobated. Though they be immemorable, they are to be corrected as corruptions of law, nor may they be allowed to revive in the future.[20] Contrary privileges, however, are not recalled.

The Council of Trent promulgated a law substantially the same as this canon, but recalling contrary privileges.[21] It follows that contrary privileges granted by the Apostolic See after the Council of Trent and still in force at

---

16 C. 1516, § 3.

17 C. 198; Vermeersch, "*Epit. Iur. Can.,*" II, 836, II.

18 Blat, "*Comment. Text Cod.,*" L. III, P. VI, 428.

19 C. 1525, § 1; "*Reprobata contraria consuetudine, administratores tam ecclesiastici quam laici cuiusvis ecclesiae etiam cathedralis aut loci pii canonice erecti aui confraternitatis, singulis annis officio tenentur reddendi rationem administrationis Ordinario loci.*"

20 C. 5.

21 Conc. Trid., Sess. XXII, de ref., Cap. 9; "*Administratores, tam eccleciastici quam laici, fabricae cujusvis ecclesiae, etiam cathedralis, hospitalis, confraternitatis, eleemosynae Montis Pietatis, et quorumcumque piorum locorum, singulis annis teneantur reddere rationem administrationis Ordinario: consuetudinibus et privilegiis quibuscumque in contrarium sublatis, nisi secus forte in institutione et ordinatione talis ecclesiae seu fabricae expresse cautum esset.*"

the time of the promulgation of the Code, retain their force by virtue of canon 4,[22] while all such privileges conceded before the Council of Trent lost their force by the promulgation of the laws of that Council.

The term "church" is general in this canon and includes all public oratories.[23] Churches, however, that belong to exempt religious are not subject to this law.[24] "*Loci pii*" signifies all ecclesiastical non-collegiate institutes canonically erected: under the term "confraternitates" falls any association legitimately erected.[25]

Consequently, this canon concerns and comprehends all the administrators of ecclesiastical goods pertaining to non-exempt moral persons.[26]

If by reason of some particular law, the account is to be rendered to others designated for this, the local Ordinary or his delegate should be admitted with these, so that an account rendered in any other manner, shall not satisfy this obligation.[27] The particular law here considered is that which may be in force from the constitution of the foundation, from civil authority or concordats.[28]

In every church a document must be drawn up recording the *onera* incurred by the acceptance of pious

---

22 Cocchi, "*Comment. in Cod.*," L. III, P. VI, 206.

23 Cfr. c. 1191, § 1.

24 Blat, "*Commentarium Textus Codicis*," L. III, P. VI, 439: "*cujusvis ecclesiae . . . sed 'saecularis, sive saecularis rector sit, sive religiosus' ad hanc norman quod attinet applicandam ex* can. 1182, § 3 . . .;" Vermeersch, "*Epitome Iuris Canonici*," II, 847; Cocchi, "*Commentarium in Codicem*." L. III, P. VI, 206.

25 Blat, "*Commentarium Text. Cod.*," L. III, P. VI, 439.

26 Cocchi, "*Commentarium in Codicem*," L. III, P. VI, 206.

27 C. 1525, § 2; "*Si ex peculiari iure aliis ad id designatis ratio reddenda sit, tunc etiam Ordinarius loci vel eius delegatus cum his admittatur, ea lege ut aliter factae liberationes ipsis administratoribus minime suffragentur.*"

28 Vermeersch, "*Epit. Iur. Can.*," II, 847; Cocchi, "*Comment. in Cod.*," L. III, P. VI, 206.

foundations.[29] The rector should keep this record in a safe place. This tablet, however, is not primary and legal evidence of the existence and conditions of a foundation, but rather a preservation of the memory of the obligations. Public proof of the fact and constitution of the foundation was treated in the last chapter.

"Church" and "rector" cannot be taken here in the strict sense of canons 1161, 1191 and 479. Ecclesiastical laws are to be understood according to the proper meaning of the words with due regard for the text and context.[30] Moral ecclesiastical persons of all kinds, not only churches, are competent to accept foundations and "church" here extends to any moral person in the Church[31] just as "rector" means the one in charge of the moral person.

This document ought to be retained in a place sufficiently protected against unlawful removal or destruction. While it does not constitute public proof of the foundation, it is the means the Church has adopted lest the pious wills of the faithful be cheated of fulfilment through forgetfulness.

Before the Code the law did not mention a safe place, but required that the tablet of Mass obligations be kept in an obvious or conspicuous place.[32]

What information should this tablet contain? Its purpose is to provide the knowledge required for the proper fulfillment of the obligations of the foundation. Consequently, it should state the number of Masses and

---

29 C. 1549, § 1.

30 C. 18.

31 Vermeersch, *"Epit. Iur. Can.,"* II, 868.

32 Innocent XII, Const. *"Nuper,"* 23 dec. 1697; Fontes 260; *"Omnes et singuli Rectores, Superiores, et Ministri quarumcumque tum Saecularium, tum Regularium Ecclesiarum, seu illarum Capitula . . . ut (onera seu Missas tum temporales tum etiam manuales) . . . quoad fieri poterit (pateant), teneantur . . . conficere, semperque in loco magis patenti, et obvio retinere Tabellam onerum perpetuorum, et temporalium Literis perspicuis, et intelligentibus descriptorum . . ."*

the amount of the stipend, together with any other requirements as to time, place and personal celebration of the Masses.

Besides the book treated in canon 843, § 1, another should be kept by the rector, in which all perpetual and temporary obligations, their fulfillment and the stipends should be noted, in order that an exact account of all these may be rendered to the Ordinary of the place.[33]

Canon 843, § 1 obliges rectors of churches and other pious places whether secular or religious, in which stipends for Masses are received, to have a special book in which they note accurately the number of Masses that have been accepted, together with the intention, stipend and celebration.[34]

The temporary *onera* of Masses to be noted in the book prescribed by canon 1549, § 2 are those arising from a foundation for a long time.[35] The term "rector" includes anyone in charge of a moral person obliged to the fulfillment of founded Masses. He must see that the notations in this book are truthful and exact, since its purpose is an exact rendition of account to the local Ordinary every year.[36]

All this is evident from the old law: "*Iidem (i. e., omnes et singuli Rectores, Superiores, et Ministri quarumcumque tum Saecularium, tum Regularium Ecclesiarum, seu illarum Capitula) teneantur pariter in Sacrario duos Libros retinere, ac in eorum altero singula onera perpetua, et temporalia, in altero autem Missas manuales, et tam illorum, quam istarum ad implementum, et*

---

[33] C. 1549, § 2; "*Pariter praeter librum de quo*" in can. 843, § 1, "*alter liber retineatur et apud rectorem servetur, in quo singula onera perpetua et temporaria eorumque implementum et eleemosynae adnotentur, ut de iis omnibus exacta ratio Ordinario loci reddatur.*"

[34] "*Rectores ecclesiarum aliorumque piorum locorum sive saecularium sive religiosorum in quibus eleemosynae Missarum recipi solent, peculiarem habeant librum in quo accurate notent Missarum receptarum numerum, intentionem, eleemosgnam, celebrationem.*"

[35] Cfr. c. 1544.

[36] C. 1525, § 1.

eleemosynas distincte, et diligenter annotare, et annotandas, seu annotanda curare, singulisque annis de supradictis adimplementis, eleemosynis, et oneribus pariter exactam rationem suis Superioribus reddere, ac omnes, et singulas rationes huiusmodi in praefatis respective Libris simili distinctione, et diligentia, tam praefati a quibus rationes debent reddi, quam Superiores, quibus reddendae erunt, describere, seu annotare, sive describendas, vel annotandas respective curare.''[37]

The decree ''*Ut debita*'' stated that, besides the tablet of perpetual *onera* and the book for the registration of manual Masses, there should be in each church, books in which were recorded perpetual obligations of Masses and their satisfaction. The Ordinary should exercise care that such books be kept.[38] The Bishop, in his visitation of the diocese and Superiors, should see that the tablet and books be kept.[39]

What legal value have this tablet and book to attest the existence and conditions of founded Masses when primary and public legal proof is lacking? The Sacred Congregation of the Council has decided that a tablet, especially if it shows signs of antiquity and veracity, merits faith and the obligations therein described must be fulfilled.[40] Indeed, obligations not even noted on the

---

37 Innocent XII, Const. "Nuper," 23 dec. 1697; Fontes, 260.

38 S. C. *Concilii, decr. "Ut debita," 11 Maii,* 1904; *Collectanea,* 2192; *"Denique officii singulorum Ordinariorum erit curare ut in singulis ecclesiis, praeter tabellam onerum perpetuorum et librum in quo manuales Missae quae a fidelibus traduntur ex ordine cum sua eleemosyna recenseantur, insuper habeantur libri in quibus dictorum onerum et Missarum satisfactio signetur. Ipsorum pariter erit vigilare super plena et omnimoda executione praesentis decreti."*

39 Gasparri, *"De Euch."* I, 568.

40 S. C. C. in Neapolitana, 10 Jan. 1665; Gasparri, *"De Euch.,"* I, 568. Cfr. *Lucidi, "De Visit. Sac. Limin.,"* II, Cap. VII, 7; S. C. *Episc. et Regul., Ripana Pii legati et delet. hypothecae,* 17 *Martii* 1854.

tablet can be established from the fact that they have been fulfilled for a long time.[41]

Moreover, the presumption is that a congruous dowry has been assigned for founded Masses inscribed on the tablet. Consequently, until the contrary is evident, there is no place for moderation but all the obligations must be carried out despite ignorance of what goods constitute the dowry.[42]

A pious and learned priest, the author of the work entitled "*Ichnographia,*" edited in 1719 at Rome, commended for the consideration of Bishops, certain cautions worthy of adoption in each diocese. His provision for the vindication and fulfillment of Mass obligations by the keeping of a tablet noting the perpetual and temporary obligations of Masses, their number, time and place of fulfillment, and indicating the testament or other legal act by which the foundation was established, were adopted and promulgated by Clement XI. The fact, however, that this tablet offered no legal proof against the public document in which the pious founder had expressed his will, was clearly recognized.[43]

The satisfaction of founded Mass obligations is proven by notation in the book kept for this purpose. When this proof is lacking, however, the Bishop can

---

[41] S. C. C. in Vercellen., 12 Sept. 1720; Perusina, 21 Jan. 1826; Gasparri, l.c. S. C. C. in Comen. *Legati Missarum,* 20 Martii, 1824; Pallottini, "*Collectio Omnium Conc. et Resol. S. C. C.,*" Tom. XIII, "*Missa,*" Sectio II.

[42] S. C. C. in *Neapolitana,* 10 Jan, 1665; Lucidi, "*De Vis. Sac. Lim.,*" II Cap. VII, 8; *"ex tom. decis. eiusdem anni testatur Crispinus de Vis. past.* P. II, Sec. 18, n. 9, *ubi resolutionem hanc ex scribit, nempe: S. C. censuit, praesumi, quod oneribus in tabella descriptis congrua dos in eorum receptione attributa fuerit, ideoque, donec de contrario non constet, non esse locum moderationi, sed esse satisfaciendum oneribus, quamvis in praesens ignoretur, quae bona fuerint assignata."*

[43] Benedict XIV, "*De Syn. Dioec.,*" Lib. XIII, Cap. Ult., 4.

upbraid priests who neglect such registration, but he cannot refuse to accept other reasonable and sufficient proof. By a statement under oath that the Masses have been celebrated, a priest merits belief, even though the inscription of the celebration was neglected.[44]

---

[44] Lucidi, "*De Vis. Sac. Lim.*," II, Cap. VII, 9; "*Monacellus, Form. leg. tit.* 13. *dorm.* 2. n. 46, *tradit, quod, 'cum Episcopus Civitatis Plebis compellere voluisset canonicos suae cathedralis ad subscribendum folium obligationis applicandi Missam conventualem pro benefactoribus, et ipsi renuendo recursum habuissent ad S. C. Conc., hac sub die* 7 *Maii* 1704, *declaravit, illos non teneri, sed sufficere illorum assertionem, se celebrasse.*"

CHAPTER VIII.

FOUNDED MASSES IN CHURCHES OF RELIGIOUS.

Authority over founded Masses has so far been conceded to the local Ordinary. The exemption of religious has not received any recognition. Before the Code, however, foundations in secular churches were subject to the Bishop, and those in churches of Regulars, to the General or Provincial of the Order.[1] Nor has the Code failed to grant authority to Superiors of exempt religious over foundations in their own churches.

In the case of pious foundations in churches, even parochial, of exempt religious, the rights and obligations of the local Ordinary from cc. 1545 to 1549 belong exclusively to the Major Superior.[2]

A church is secular if it does not belong to a religious institute or family, *i. e.*, if it is not among the goods of a religious institute or family.[3] A secular church which is given over to the care of religious, is not a religious church in the sense of this canon, and foundations in it are subject to the Ordinary of the place.

That the Major Superior hold the place of the local Ordinary in canons 1545 to 1549, the one requirement is that the foundation be established in a church of exempt religious. It makes no difference whether the religious institute be clerical or lay.

This offers an explanation why one finds canon 1550 in the Code rather than the term "*Ordinarius*" in canons 1545 to 1549. Had the term "*Ordinarius*" been substituted in these canons for "*Ordinarius loci,*" the Major Superior of an exempt lay institute would have been deprived of authority over foundations in churches of that institute. The term "*Ordinarius*" applies only to major

---

[1] Innocent XII, Const. "*Nuper,*" 23 dec. 1679: Fontes, 260.

[2] C. 1550: "*Si agatur de piis fundationibus in ecclesiis, etiam paroecialibus, religiosorum exemptorum, iura et officia Ordinarii loci, de quibus* in can. 1545-1549, exclusive *competunt Superiori maiori.*"

[3] Blat, "*Comment. Text. Cod. Iur. Can.,*" Lib. III, P. II, 33.

Superiors of exempt clerical religious institutes.[4] The legislator intended to grant power over foundations in their churches to Major Superiors of all exempt religious institutes, whether clerical or lay; hence canon 1550. Blat appears to fall into error on this point when he indicates that Major Superior is synonymous in this canon with "Ordinary."[5]

A Major Superior is a Prime Abbot, the Abbot Superior of a Monastic Congregation, the Abbot of a Monastery "*sui iuris,*" even if it belong to a Monastic Congregation, the Supreme Moderator of a religious institute, the Provincial Superior, the Vicars of these and others who enjoy power "*ad instar provincialium.*"[6]

Religious, even though exempt, are bound by the decree of the local Ordinary or the diocesan custom regarding the manual stipend.[7] What of the founded stipend established by the local Ordinary? Is this also binding upon exempt religious?

In virtue of canons 1550 and 1545, Major Superiors of exempt religious have the right to establish the minimum dowry that may be accepted for a foundation in their churches. Neither canon 831 nor canon 1545 grants authority expressly for the establishment of a founded stipend. The difficulty must be solved by discovering whether the power of establishing the founded stipend flows from authority over the manual stipend or from authority over the quantity of the dowry for a foundation. Surely, one who vindicates to himself the right to determine the founded stipend, practically claims the right to establish the quantity of the dowry for a founda-

---

[4] C. 198, § 1.

[5] Blat, *Comment. Text. Cod. Iur. Can.,*" Lib. III, P. VI, 468: "*iura et officia Ordinarii loci de quibus* in can. 1545-1549, exclusive *competunt Superiori maiori cuilibet, qui 'in iure nomine Ordinarii pro suis subditis intelligitur'* (c. 198 § 1)."

[6] C. 488, 8°.

[7] C. 831, § 2.

tion. For a founded stipend is determined precisely that one may be able to judge the quantity of the dowry required to care for the celebration of the number of Masses requested. Hence he who determines the founded stipend determines the requisite dowry. The Major Superior of exempt religious, then, is not bound by the local founded stipend because he has authority over the amount of the dowry for founded Masses. The authority of the local Ordinary over the manual stipend does not militate against this conclusion because the manual stipend is determined without the provision for the future required for founded Masses.

The exclusive right to invest the dowry of a foundation in all churches of exempt religious belongs to the Major Superior of the religious institute.[8] By canon 533, however, the Superior or Superioress of a house of a religious Congregation must obtain the previous consent of the local Ordinary for the investment of money given to the house as a legacy for the worship of God to be used in that very place. Moreover, any religious, though he be a regular, *i. e.*, a member of an Order, must obtain this same consent if the money was given to a parish or mission, or to the religious because of a parish or mission.[9]

If a gift to the house of a religious Congregation is a foundation for Masses to be celebrated in that very place, the investment of the dowry falls under the terms of canon 533, for it is "*ad Dei cultum . . . . eo ipso loco impendendam.*" As a foundation for Masses, if the

---

[8] CC. 1550, 1547.

[9] C. 533, § 1. "*Pro pecuiae quoque collocattione servetur praescriptum* can. 532, 1; *sed praeviem consensum Ordinarii loci obtinere teneantur:*

3°. *Superior vel Antistita domus Congregationis religiosae, si qui fundi domui tributi legative sint ad Dei cultum beneficentiamve eo ipso loco impendendam:*

4°. *Religiosus quilibet, etsi Ordinis regularis alumnus, si pecunia data sit paroeciae vel missioni, aut religiosis intuitu paroeciae vel missionis.*"

house were of an exempt religious Congregation, the investment of the endowment would fall under canons 1550, 1547. The latter canons would grant exclusive right of investment to the Major Superior of the exempt religious Congregation, while canon 533 would require previous consent of the local Ordinary. Here is evidently a conflict. How must reconciliation be effected?

An opinion of Vermeersch that canon 533, § 1, 3° does not apply to exempt clerical religious Congregations, would end the conflict.[10] The author unwarrantedly limits his opinion to exempt clerical religious Congregations. By c. 1550, exempt lay religious Congregations are as independent of the local Ordinary as exempt clerical religious Congregations. His arguments apply equally to all exempt Congregations, whether clerical or lay.

According to this opinion, canon 533, § 1, 3° does not clash with canons 1550, 1547. If canon 533, § 1, 3° does not apply to exempt religious, then canons 1550, 1547 govern the investment of the dowry of founded Masses in churches of exempt religious, and canon 533, § 1, 3° does not apply to such a foundation.

The arguments of the author do not appear sufficiently strong to demand acceptance. Should Vermeersch's opinion be accepted, the difficulty is dispelled. On the other hand, should his opinion be rejected, the difficulty must be resolved by the same argumentation as that employed in the reconciliation of c. 533, § 1, 4°, which surely applies to all exempt religious institutes, with canons 1550, 1547.

---

[10] Vermeersch, "*Epit. Iur.* Can.," I, 606; "*Obligatio ista* (*i. e., the obligation of previous consent from the local Ordinary*) *est propria Congregationum religiosarum. Non pertinet itaque ad Ordines religiosos; neque, ut arbitramur, ad Congregationes clericales exemptas, quae, ex.* c. 1550, *pro cultu in suis ecclesiis non magis quam regulares pendent ad Ordinario loci. Ceterum verba: 'etiam exemptae' quae, v. g. ponuntur* c. 512, § 2, 2°, *hic desiderantur.*"

In cc. 1550, 1547, the right to invest the endowment of a foundation in a church of exempt religious, is granted exclusively to the Major Superior. The term "exclusive" appears to preclude the application of c. 533, § 1, 3° and 4° to the investment of a dowry for founded Masses. The reason, however, why the previous consent of the local Ordinary is required by 3° and 4° seems to be that the gift was primarily in view of the place and for the benefit of that place. This consideration may have led the legislator to require the previous consent of the local Ordinary for the investment of such gifts.

The use of the term "exclusive" in c. 1550 and the fact that that canon is specifically for foundations while canon 533, § 1, 3° and 4° extends also to other cases than foundations, seem to render juridically more probable the opinion that c. 533, § 1, 3° and 4° does not apply to foundations.

All religious institutes, whether exempt or not, are bound by the right of the local Ordinary to knowledge concerning the administration of "*fundi*" (money or immovable fruitful goods or other goods to be converted into money),[11] or legacies concerning which c. 533, § 1, 3° and 4° treats.[12] As explained above, this rendition of account may apply to foundations for Masses.

An official document of a foundation for Masses in churches of exempt religious is required in the archive of the moral person and also in the archive of the Major Superior of the religious institute. Canon 1548, § 2 uses the phrase "*in Curiae archivo*" but canon 1550 makes it a legitimate inference that either the provincial archive or that of the Abbot of a monastery "*sui iuris*" is the

---

11 Vermeersch, "*Epit. Iur.* Can." I, 606.

12 C. 535, § 3, 2°: "*Loci Ordinario ius insuper esto cognoscendi: De administratione fundorum legatorumque de quibus* in can. 533, 1, nn. 3, 4.": *Fanfani, "De Iure Religiosorum,"* 173.

proper place for the record of founded Masses in churches of exempt religious.[13]

The right of vigilance over the execution of founded Masses in churches of exempt religious belongs exclusively to the Major Superior. To him must other delegated executors render account.[14]

Since by common law power to reduce Masses is granted only by indult from the Apostolic See, one need only note here that recourse for such an indult or for an individual reduction is conceded for Masses founded in churches of religious or transferred to their churches, by Sacred Congregation for Religious.[15]

---

[13] Fanfani, "*De Iure Religiosorum*," 172.

[14] C. 1515; Fanfani, "*De Iure Religiosorum*," 174.

[15] A. A. S., XI, 251; "*Utrum concedere, servatis consuetis normis sanationes et condonationes quoad praeteritum, et reductiones quoad futurum relate ad capellanias et alia legata, quae, licet concredita non sint Ordini aut familiae religiosae, qua talis, erecta tamen aut translata reperiuntur in ecclesiis religiosorum, spectet ad S. C. Concilii, an potius ad S. C. de Religiosis.*

Eminentissimi Patres Cardinales, quibus a SSmo. D. N. Benedicto PP. XV resolutio comissa fuit, respondendum censuerunt:

Privative ad S. C. de Religiosis, quoadusque legatorum administratio et adimplementum concredita sint Religiosis.

Quae omnia SSmus D. N. rata habuit et confirmavit.

Romae, die 24 *Martii* 1919."

CHAPTER IX.

Reduction, Translation, Condonation of Founded Masses.

That Canon Law guarantees the fulfillment of founded Masses as far as possible, has been amply demonstrated. Despite this solicitude, the fact remains that complete and certain fore-knowledge of the future is beyond the power of the human intellect and circumstances at times render practically impossible the carrying out of obligations that have been assumed. The limitations of human knowledge require legislation for the reduction of founded Masses.

These laws, however, so restrict the power of reduction that they lend additional evidence of the faithfulness of Church legislation in protecting pious bequests from fraud.

Reduction of founded Masses is reserved to the Apostolic See even in those cases when Ordinaries are permitted to reduce other foundations. The will of the founder, expressed in the official document of the foundation, is the one source whence Ordinaries gain authority to reduce founded Masses. Indults to Bishops for the reduction of founded obligations are to be strictly interpreted, so that a general indult for reducing the *onera* of a pious foundation is not extended to founded Masses without explicit mention of such extension. Nor is an indult for reducing founded Masses to be extended to manual or "*ad instar manualium*" Masses, of the same foundation.[1]

The obligation of Masses must always be fulfilled unless it ceases of itself from intrinsic reasons or is reduced or extinguished by legitimate authority for a just cause.[2]

The onus of founded Masses ceases of itself by the expiration of the time specified as a limit to the obligation. Thus a foundation requiring Masses for fifty years does not urge when the fifty years have elapsed. This is evident, but when the foundation is perpetual, can the passage of time of itself extinguish the obligation?

Some formerly held that no foundation for Masses perdured beyond ten years. This opinion, however, was proven altogether false and was condemned by Alexander VII on the 18th of March, 1666.[3] This opinion was occa-

---

[1] C. 1551: § 1. "*Reductio onerum quae pias fundationes gravant, uni Sedi Apostolicae reservatur, nisi in tabulis fundationis aliud expresse caveatur, et salvo praescripto* can. 1517, 2.

§ 2. *Indultum reducendi Missas fundatas non protenditur nec ad alias Missas ex contractu debitas, nec ad alia onera piae fundationis.*

§ 3. *Indultum vero generale reducendi onera piarum fundationum ita intelligendum est, nisi aliud constet, ut indultarius potius alia onera quam Missas reducat.* C. 1517: 2. "*Si tamen exsecutio onerum impositorum, ob imminutos reditus aliamve causam, nulla administratorum culpa, impossibilis evaserit, tunc Ordinarius quoque, auditis iis quorum interest, et servata, meliore quo fieri potest modo, fundatoris voluntate, poterit eadem onera aeque imminuere excepta Missarum reductione quae semper Sedi Apostolicae unice competit.*"

[2] Cfr. c. 1514.

[3] The condemned proposition was: "*Annuum legatum pro anima relictum non durat plus quam per decem annos.*" Denzinger, "*Enchiridion Symbolorum et Definitionum,*" 1143.

sioned by D. Soto, who believed that none remains in purgatory for twenty years: indeed, not even for ten years.[4]

Neither ten years nor any other time has been recognized as terminating the obligation of Masses founded as perpetual, but the question of prescription against founded Masses has given rise to a difference of opinion among canonists and moralists.

Without a shadow of doubt, under the Code, prescription cannot prevail against founded Masses.[5] This canon evidently excludes not only ordinary prescription but also centenary and immemorable. Neither has prescription any power to induce a change in the number of Masses, their quality or place of celebration.[6]

Before the Code, many thought that prescription against founded Masses was possible, although they did not agree concerning the requisite time.[7] Since prescription was admitted by canon law, they saw no reason why the obligations of Masses should be excluded.[8] Others denied this, alleging many reasons—that good faith could not easily be presumed; that prescription against one who could not act, is repugnant to natural equity; that negligence should not be the foundation for retention of the income without fulfilling the obliga-

---

4 Cappello, "*De Sac.*" I. 718, (12): "*Causa seu occasio huius opinionis fuit sententia D. Soti, qui* (lib. IV, dist. 19, q. 2, a. 2) *dicit*: '*Quapropter crediderim numquam aliquem in purgatorio viginti annis extilisse, imo, ut mea fert opinio, nec decem. Nam cum nemo illic sit nisi Dei amicus, contritio eius, et, post Christum passum, sacramenta et suffragia et bona quae agit opera, ad cumulum ei satisfactionis accedunt.*'"

5 C. 1509; "*Praescriptioni obnoxia non sunt*: 5°. *Eleemosynae et onera Missarum.*"

6 Cappello, "*De Sac.,*" I. 719, 2.

7 Pasqualigo, *De Sacrificio Novae Legis, Questiones Theologicae, Morales, Juridicae.*" Tom. II. Quest. 1192: Tamburnini. "*De Sacrificio Missae,*" Lib. III. Cap. VII. 1.

8 S. Alphonsus, "*Theologia Moralis.*" VI, 324.

tions.[9] Saint Alphonsus says, however, that the strongest argument for the latter position was from the Council of Trent: "*Ratio postulat ut illis quae bene constituta sunt, contrariis ordinationibus non detrahatur. Quando igitur ex beneficiorum quorumcumque erectione seu fundatione aut aliis constitutionibus, qualitates aliquae requiruntur, seu certa illis onera sunt injuncta; id beneficiorum collatione, seu in quacumque alia dispositione, eis non derogetur . . .: et aliter facta provisio surreptitia censeatur.*"[10]

Many responses of the Sacred Congregation of the Council confirm this latter opinion.[11] Gasparri considers one of these responses sufficient evidence of the attitude of that Congregation:[12] "*S. C. C. in Lucana*, 18 *Febr.* 1702: '*Agebatur de capellania quam fundator erigi mandaverat pro amore Dei et remedio animae suae, et capellanum designaverat qui Missam singulo mane celebrare curaret. Quamvis capellani pro tempore sacrificium applicare a saeculo et amplius omisissent, probante etiam episcopo in sacra visitatione, tamen S. C. declaravit capellanum teneri Missam applicare juxta fundatoris intentionem.*' "[13]

The obligation of founded Masses no longer urges, if the dowry fails without fault of the administrator,[14] for a perpetual onus of Masses is accepted in view of a certain dowry, the revenue from which is considered sufficient to provide for the expenses of fulfillment. The gift is because of the duty, and it is just that the duty

---

9 Gasparri, *"De Euch.,"* I, 567: S. Alphonsus, *"Theologia Mor.,"* VI, 324: Lucidi, *"De Vis. Sac. Lim.,"* Cap. VII, 11: Wernz, *"Jus Decretalium,"* III, 206, 300.

10 Sess. XXV, de ref. Cap. 5.

11 Cfr. Pallottini, *"Collectio Omnium, etc.,"* tom. XIII, *Missa*, par. 2, 47 *seqq.*

12 *"De Euch.,"* I, 567.

13 Cfr. Lucidi, *"De Vis. Sacr. Lim.,"* Cap. VII. 13.

14 Gasparri, *"De Euch.,"* I, 588.

ceases when the gift is lost or perish.[15] As Cappello says, the obligation of celebrating such Masses is present only in so much as a sufficient stipend is received and if the dowry perish, the stipend is no longer received, the obligation consequently ceasing. If, however, the deficiency is culpable, the church or institute is by no means relieved of the obligation of celebrating the Masses.[16]

The same principles hold for the loss of the income, for the income, not the dowry itself, is the source of the stipends. The obligation ceases only if the loss of the income were inculpable.[17]

The Sacred Congregation of the Council declared that certain chaplains and holders of benefices were not obliged to celebrate Masses for the founders of the chaplaincies or benefices while the dowry was inculpably fruitless.[18] The same Congregation decreed on the 15th of Sept., 1657, that, as long as the dowry was not invested fruitfully, the ecclesiastical institute was not held to the celebration of Masses from its own income.

What if the income from the dowry is diminished without fault? Does the obligation diminish intrinsically or must legitimate authority intervene?

If the founder has not specified the number of Masses, the solution is evident. As many Masses must be celebrated as there are stipends from the income, for the number of Masses is determined on the basis of the stipend specified by the founder, or in defect of this, on the basis of the diocesan stipend.[19] Such a diminution

---

15 Schmalzgrueber, *"Jus Ecclesiasticum Universum,"* Tom. III, Pars. III, Tit. XLI, 137; Wernz, *"Jus Decretalium,"* III. 206: S. C. C. 20 Dec., 1879.

16 Cappello, *"De Sac.,"* I, 718.

17 Cappello, l.c., 718.

18 S. C. C. Monopolitana, 8 Aug., 1705; Forosempronien, 7 Junii, 1686.

19 C. 830; *"Si quis pecuniae summam obtulerit pro Missarum applicatione, non indicans earumdem numerum, his supputetur secundum eleemosynam loci in quo oblator morabatur, nisi aliam fuisse ejus intentionem legitime praesumi debeat."*

is in full accord with the will of the founder and there is no need for reductive authority.

If the quality of the Masses, solemn, high or low, has not been settled by the founder, legitimate presumptions must be used. For example, the founder may reasonably be presumed to have desired high Masses if such was his customary request or if high Masses were customary in his locality.

In his dissertation, "Mass Stipends," Father Keller[20] embraces the opinion that a founder may generally be presumed to have desired solemn or high Masses rather than low Masses because the Church prefers solemn or high Masses to low Masses. If it is a legitimate presumption that the founder's will coincides with the Church's preference, Father Keller's opinion would be tenable; for the will of the founder determines the quality of the Masses as well as the other obligations involved in the acceptance of the endowment. The Church, however, does not forbid the celebration of low Masses. Hence, low Masses might legitimately be requested and the custom of the founder or his locality would seem a more correct index of his will than the mind of the Church, of which he may not even have been aware. The fact that he would have desired solemn or high Masses had he known the mind of the Church, can hardly of itself justify the celebration of solemn Masses, especially if he was accustomed to have low Masses celebrated during his lifetime.

Should, however, the founder determine the number of Masses, a reduction of the number must be obtained from the Apostolic See.[21] The opinion of those who held that reduction in such a case did not require authority

---

20 P. 85, sqq.
21 CC. 1517, § 2, 1551, § 1.

of the Apostolic See, today is untenable.[22] This case is one of reduction of Masses, which will be treated a little later in this same chapter.

The cessation of founded Masses from intrinsic causes has been discussed. These cases require no intervention of reductive authority; the causes are effective of themselves. At times, however, unforeseen circumstances may render the fulfillment of these *onera* practically impossible, as when monetary values so change that the income is altogether insufficient. Then the obligation still urges, and the intervention of legitimate authority alone can effect a reduction. This use of the term "reduction" is the same as that in canon 1551.

Benedict XIV[23] points out very clearly the improper use of the term "reduction of Masses," *i. e.*, a diminution of their number. This illustrious canonist uses the method of examples to clarify the distinction.

If the will of the testator is not clearly expressed in a legacy for Masses, the decision which specifies the obligations, is improperly termed a reduction of Masses. This is a determination, not a reduction. In like manner, the release from an obligation imposed by the testator without a sufficient endowment, is not a reduction in a strict sense. So, too, the term "reduction" would be faultily used of the extinction of founded Masses by the expiration of the time stipulated by the founder for the fulfillment of the obligation. The above cases are not reductions, but declarations that the onus was never legitimately imposed, or that it ceased intrinsically.

Benedict XIV, in his Constitution "*Paternae solicitudinis,*" of the year 1749, conceded to the Friars "Minimi" of St. Francis de Paul, that perpetual *onera* of Masses in their churches should not bind after fifty years. Some thought these obligations ceased by pon-

22 Cappello, "*De Sac.,*" I, 718.
23 "*De Synod. Dioeces.,*" Lib. XIII, Cap. Ult., 8.

tifical indult, but Cappello holds it more correct to state that they ceased by consent of the founders to the first condition required by the above Constitution of the Friars, namely, that those who wished to establish perpetual Masses in their churches should be notified of the cessation of these foundations after fifty years.[24] His position is the correct one because Benedict XIV cites this case as an example of the improper use of the term "reduction of Masses."[25] These obligations ceased, not by pontifical indult, but intrinsically by the founders' consent to a time limit of fifty years. This indult is still in force.[26]

Reduction of Masses in a strict sense, as employed in canon 1551, is defined by Cappello as "the act of competent authority by which the number of Masses prescribed by the founder is reduced for a just cause."[27] Reduction refers to the future, and has reference only to those Masses yet to be celebrated; for concerning those Masses, the celebration of which has been neglected, there is no place for reduction but only "condonation."

The same author continues:[28] "Condonation is absolution given by competent authority from past omissions either of manual or founded Masses the due celebration of which was neglected. Consequently condonation, in contrast to reduction, has respect to the past. By virtue of condonation or absolution, a priest is relieved in conscience, i. e., before God and the Church, of his obligations in regard to Masses that he has neglected to celebrate."[29]

---

24 Cappello, "*De Sac.,*" I, 718, (17).

25 Benedict XIV, "*De Syn. Dioec.,*" Lib. XIII, Cap. Ult., 9.

26 Cappello, "*De Sac.,*" I, 718, (17).

27 "*Reductionis nomine hic venit actus auctoritatis competentis, quo numerus Missarum praescriptus a fundatore vel ab offerente eleemosynas manuales justa de causa imminuitur.*"; ("*De Sac.,*" I, 720).

28 Cappello, l.c.

29 "*Condonatio est absolutio data ab auctoritate competente super praeteritis omissionibus Missarum sive manualium sive fundatarum, quae celebrari debuissent et celebratae non fuerunt.;*" (Cappello, l.c., 721).

Benedict XIV makes the same distinction: "Condonations or remissions—requests for remission or condonation of Masses not celebrated, for which the stipend has been received—are called by some reductions of Masses, but less correctly since these cases refer only to past time. Reductions properly so-called, look to the future."[30]

Another modification of the obligations of founded Masses by legitimate authority is the translation of Masses. Translations concern either the place or time of celebration and consist in the faculty conceded by an ecclesiastical Superior by which permission is granted for the celebration of Masses at another time or in another place than that determined by the founder.[31] This is a reduction, not regarding the number of Masses to be celebrated but regarding some incidental obligation imposed by the founder. Hence it may be looked upon as a sort of minor reduction, accidental rather than substantial.

Reductions, condonations and translations in the sense explained above, are effected by the intervention of proper authority when the fulfillment of the express will of the founder is interfered with by unforeseen circumstances. The cessation of a founded obligation otherwise is due either to the invalidity of the foundation, to its nullification by a total and inculpable loss of revenue or dowry, or to expiration of the time determined in its

30 *"Hujusmodi quoque condonationes, sive remissiones,—instantiae ad obtinendam remissionem seu condonationem Missarum non celebratarum, pro quibus tamen recepta est eleemosyna . . . — ab aliquibus dicuntur reductiones Missarum; sed minus recte, et omnino improprie: quum hae praeteritum tempus solummodo respiciant; verae autem, et propriae dictae reductiones futuro tempori provideant.;"* (*"De Syn. Dioec.,"* Lib. XIII, Cap. Ult., 13).

31 *"Translatio respicere potest sive locum sive tempus celebrationis, et consistit in facultate concessa a Superiore ecclesiastico, qua indulgetur ut Missas quae determinato tempore et loco celebrandae essent, alio tempore et loco celebrentur.;"* (Cappello, *"Tract. Can.—Mor. de Sac.,"* I, 722).

constitution. The term reduction is employed strictly in canon 1551, which is now considered.

Reduction of the obligations which are incumbent upon pious foundations, is reserved to the Apostolic See alone, unless it is otherwise expressly provided in the official document of the foundation, saving also the prescription of canon 1517, 2.[32]

This latter canon—1517, § 2—grants no faculties for the reduction of Masses, which it states are always reserved to the Apostolic See alone.[33]

Reduction of founded Masses is permitted by common law to authority inferior to the Apostolic See only when the founder has expressed such a concession in the official foundation document. A reduction made otherwise than by authority of the Apostolic See, even for a most grave cause, is by law null and void.[34]

On the 21st of June, 1625, the Congregation of the Council published by special authority of Urban VIII, the decree "*Cum Saepe contingat:*"[35] *Ac primo districte prohibet atque interdicit (S C C) ne Episcopi in dioecesana Synodo aut Generales in Capitulis generalibus, vel aliis, quoquo modo reducant onera ulla Missarum celebrandarum, aut post idem Concilium imposita aut in limine fundationis, sed pro his omnibus reducendis aut moderandis vel commutandis ad Apostolicam Sedem recurratur, quae, re diligenter perspecta, id statuet quod magis in Domino expedire arbitrabitur; alioquin, reduc-*

---

[32] C. 1551, § 1; "*Reductio onerum quae pias fundationes gravant, uni Sedi Apostolicae reservatur, nisi in tabulis fundationis aliud expresse caveatur, et salvo praescripto* can. 1517, § 2."

[33] C. 1517, § 2; "*Si tamen exsecutio onerum impositorum, ob imminutos reditus aliamve causam, nulla administratorum culpa, impossibilis evaserit, tunc Ordinarius quoque, auditis iis quorum interest, et servata, meliore quo fieri potest modo, fundatoris voluntate, poterit eadem onera aeque imminuere, excepta Missarum reductione quae semper Sedi Apostolicae unice competit.*"

[34] Cappello, "*De Sac.,*" I, 720.

[35] Collectanea, 16.

tiones.. moderationes et commutationes huiusmodi, si quas contra hujus prohibitionis formam fieri contigerit, omnino nullas atque inanes decernit."

Authentic interpretation of the above was given on the 23rd of December, 1697, by Innocent XII:[36] *Super primo Sacrae Congregationis Decreto de celebratione Missarum, quo prohibetur, ne Episcopi in Diocesana Synodo, aut Generales in Capitulis Generalibus, vel alias quoquo modo, reducant onera illa Missarum celebrandarum, aut post idem Concilium imposita, aut in limine fundationis. Quaeritur, quid si legatum sit ita tenue, ut non sit, qui velit onus illi iniunctum subire, et si recurrendum sit ad Apostolicam Sedem pro moderatione oneris, totum, aut fere totum insumendum sit pro expensis ad id necessariis? Et quid, si permittatur Episcopo in fundatione, ut possit huiusmodi onera moderari.*

"Sacra Congregatio Cardinalium Concilii Tridentini Interpretum, auctoritate sibi a Sanctissimo Domino nostro attributa . . . ad hunc modum respondit, videlicet:

Ad primum. Et si legatum sit adeo tenue, nihilominus pro reductione oneris, ut supra, impositi, ab iis, ad quos pertinet, Sedem Apostolicam esse adeundam, quae absque ulla impensa id statuet quod magis in Domino e re esse iudicaverit; verumtamen, si in ipsa Beneficii erectione expresse cautum fuerit, ut liceat Episcopo iniunctum onus reducere, et moderari, legem hanc fundationis, quam Decreta hac de re edita non sustulerunt, esse validam, et observandam."

This extensive quotation has been given verbatim because the Code does not depart from this legislation. The question agitated by authors[37] before the Code

[36] Const. "*Nuper;*" Fontes, 260.

[37] Cfr. S. Alphonsus, "*Theologia Mor.,*" Lib. VI, 331; Gennari. "*Consultazioni Morali—Canoniche—Liturgiche,*" Vol. II, p. 15, 8, 1; Tamburini, "*De Sacrificio Missae Expedite Celebrando,*" Lib. III, Cap. I, 2, 2; Lucidi, "*De Vis. Sac. Lim.,*" Cap. VII, 78, sqq.; Gasparri, "*De Euch.,*" I, 588: Wernz, "*Jus Decretalium,*" III, 207; Benedict XIV, "*De Syn. Dioec.,*" Lib. XIII, Cap. Ult., 17 sqq.

whether a Bishop could reduce Masses when the income, at first sufficient, had been inculpably reduced so that it was incapable of supplying stipends for the Masses, has been decided by the Code. Canon 1517 § 2 reserved to the Apostolic See the reduction of the number of founded Masses determined by the founder because of reduced revenue, unless such permission has been expressly conceded to the Ordinary by the founder.

Cappello says that the reduction of Masses exceeds ordinary Episcopal power, and is exclusively reserved to the Apostolic See because it implies suppletion of the satisfying fruit from the treasure of the Church. The satisfaction of Christ and the Saints is applied for those for whom the Masses ought to be offered.[38] The impetratory fruit is supplied from the prayer of the Church.[39] Because of this suppletion, those for whom the Masses should be applied suffer no injury.[40] None is ignorant that the Roman Pontiff alone can supply from the treasury of the Church.

An Ordinary, unless he has been granted reductive power by the founder, can reduce Masses only by virtue of an Apostolic Indult. Has the Apostolic See been accustomed to grant such indults?

The Fathers of the Council of Trent discovered that the existing condition of founded Masses called for remedy. Foundations for Masses were too numerous for fulfillment. Frequently the constituted stipend was so slight that no priest was willing to accept it.[41]

These conditions evoked the following decree: '*Sancta Synodus, cupiens haec ad pios usus relicta, quo plenius et utilius potest, impleri, facultatem dat episcopis ut in synodo dioecesana, itemque abbatibus et generalibus ordinum, ut in suis capitulis generalibus, re diligenter*

---

38 Cappello, *"De Sacr.,"* 1, 720, 4.
39 Benedict XIV, *"De Syn. Dioec.,"* Lib. XIII, Cap. Ult., 15.
40 Pasqualigo, *"De Sacr. Nov. Leg.,"* Quest. 1152, 3.
41 Benedict XIV, *"De Syn. Dioec.,"* Lib. XIII, Cap. Ult., 18.

perspecta, possint pro sua conscientia, in praedictis ecclesiis, quas hac provisione indigere cognoverint, statuere circa haec quidquid magis ad Dei honorem et cultum, atque ecclesiarum utilitatem viderint expedire; ita tamen ut eorum semper defunctorum commemoratio fiat, qui pro suarum animarum salute legata ea ad pios usus reliquerunt."[42]

These faculties for the reduction of Masses were extremely limited, as is evident from the decree of the Sacred Congregation of the Council of the 15th of December, 1629.[43] They gave authority for reduction only in the first diocesan Synod held after the Council of Trent and only for obligations already imposed before that same Council.[44] Interest in them is historical except as an evidence of the jealous safeguarding of the power of reduction by the Apostolic See, an attitude that perdures today.

One could hardly say how great a variety of questions were submitted to the Congregation of the Council because of the reservation of the reduction of Masses. To gain relief from some of these burdensome details, that Council frequently delegated to Bishops the faculty of reducing Masses in their dioceses. With this faculty, however, was given also an instruction regarding the proper process of reduction.[45]

The mind of the Congregation of the Council in granting faculties for reduction of Masses was that the grant did not extend to other founded obligations, such as the distribution of alms to the poor. Even when the

---

[42] Conc. Trid., Sess. XXV, de ref. c. 4.

[43] Cfr. Pallottini, "*Collectio Omn. Conclus., etc.,*" Tom. XIV, *Missa*, XI, 5; " . . . *censuit, facultatem reducendi onera Missarum, tributam Episcopis ex decreto* cap. 4, sess. 25, *de reformatione, intelligi tantum de prima Synodo post idem Concilium celebrata, ac de oneribus Missarum celebrandarum ante idem Concilium impositis.*"; Benedict XIV, "*De Syn. Dioec.,*" Lib. XIII, Cap. Ult., 18.

[44] Wernz, "*Jus Decretalium.,*" III, 207.

[45] Benedict XIV, "*De Syn. Dioec.,*" Lib. XIII, Cap. Ult., 20.

Instruction contained such a phrase as "*pia legata, et Missarum onera,*" a study of the document furnished sufficient evidence that the faculties were limited to Masses. This limitation of faculties is founded on that "*regula juris*" which teaches that a faculty given for certain things, ought not to be extended to other things of a different kind.[46]

In the Code, one finds a law that an indult for the reduction of founded Masses extends neither to other Masses due by contract nor to other *onera* of the pious foundation.[47]

The other Masses due by contract may be either manual or "*ad instar manualium.*" The long duration of founded obligations furnish opportunity for fluctuating conditions to render a reduction imperative, a condition to which manual or "*ad instar manualium*" Masses are not so readily subject. For this reason, founded Masses may at times be reduced, when manual or "*ad instar manualium*" Masses are not reduced because inability to celebrate these latter Masses is not so easily subject to the plea of inculpability.

A general indult for the reduction of the *onera* of pious foundations is to be understood, unless there be evidence to the contrary, so that he who has obtained the indult, reduces other obligations rather than Masses.[48]

This canon is in accordance with the practice of the Sacred Congregation of the Council before the Code. If a foundation for Masses together with other pious works, such as the distribution of alms, required reduc-

---

46 Benedict XIV, l.c., 22.

47 C. 1551, § 2; "*Indultum reducendi Missas fundatas non protenditur nec ad alias Missas ex contractu debitas nec ad alia onera piae fundationis.*"

48 C. 1551, § 3; "*Indultum vero generale reducendi onera piarum fundationum ita intelligendum est, nisi aliud constet, ut indultarius potius alia onera quam Missas reducat.*"

tion because of diminution of revenue, the other *onera* were diminished rather than the Masses.[49]

Benedict XIV cites two cases when the reduction of Masses may take precedence over the reduction of the other obligations of a foundation. If part of the dowry has been assigned for the celebration of Masses, and the income from that part alone fails, the Masses might be reduced, the other obligations remaining. A similar reduction might be granted when the context of the foundation indicates the founder's preference for a reduction of Masses. These apparent exceptions are founded on a presumption that the founder would rather have the number of Masses diminished, a presumption which admits direct proof to the contrary.[50]

One who has obtained an indult for reduction of Masses, ought not to proceed while there remains a question whether the Masses or the other obligations of the foundation should be reduced. He should consult the Congregation of the Council and await a decision.[51] An indult for the reduction of Masses extends to anniversary Masses, solemn Masses and Masses with chant. An extention, however, to Masses due by contract, is not legitimate. This restriction of the Code in c. 1551, is in accordance with the Instruction on the use of faculties to reduce Masses under the old law: "*Exceptis instrumentis, seu contractibus, super quibus manus apponere non debeat, nisi in casu judiciali instantiae pro illorum rescissione, titulo laesionis.*"[52]

The practice of the Sacred Congregation of the Council regarding indults for the reduction of Masses can

---

[49] Benedict XIV, "*De Syn. Dioec.,*" Lib. XIII, Cap. Ult., 23; Cfr. *Fagnanus in cap. ex parte, n.* 34 *de constitutionibus;* Cfr. also S. C. C., June, 1586, *Ep. Cremonensi,* Lib. 4 decret, pp. 161 & 162; "*Quatenus ab habente potestatem reductio facienda sit, reducendas potius eleemosynas, quam missas.*"

[50] Benedict XIV, l.c.

[51] Benedict XIV, l.c., 24.

[52] Benedict XIV, l.c., 25.

be gathered from the above observations of Benedict XIV. Since the Code has introduced no change in this legislation, the constant "stylus" of this Congregation is of considerable value.

Correct procedure in questions concerning the reduction of Masses presupposes knowledge of the legitimate causes for reduction and the circumstances in which reduction has place. One ignorant of these details would be inviting troublesome investigations if he were to proceed to reduce Masses,[53] for reduction is conceded only for a just and necessary cause.[54]

Diminution of the income from the dowry is practically always required for reduction. This diminution is taken here in reference to the stipends which the income must supply; if the income should decrease but still be capable of supplying stipends for the required number of Masses, there is not sufficient cause for reduction. A lowering of monetary values or an increase in the diocesan stipend might make the income insufficient without the fruitfulness of the dowry becoming deficient. In this case, the revenue would remain the same, but an increase of the demands upon it would render it insufficient.[55]

The conditions of the foundation should be carefully studied before the sufficiency of a cause for reduction is decided. At times the testator imposes a legitimate obligation on his heir to supply any deficiency in the income. In that case, the heir should be warned to fulfill his obligation, and the Masses should not be reduced unless the heir fails in his duty. The Sacred Congregation of

---

[53] Benedict XIV, l.c., 27.

[54] Conc. Trident., de ref., sess. XXII, c. 6; Cfr. Cappello, *"De Sac.,"* I, 720, 6.

[55] Gasparri, *"De Euch.,"* I, 620; Benedict XIV, *"De Syn. Dioec.,"* Lib. XIII, Cap. Ult., 28; Cfr. Conc. Trident., de ref., sess. XXV, c. 4; Barbosa, *"De Officio et Potestate Episcopi,"* Par. II, Alleg. XXIX; S. Alphonsus, *"Theol. Mor.,"* Lib. VI, 331.

the Council decided that the obligation imposed by testament on the heir of having a certain number of Masses celebrated for the testator, was not finally fulfilled by a foundation for those Masses. An inculpable reduction of the income would oblige the heir to supply the funds requisite for the celebration of the stipulated number of Masses.[56]

Should the testator, however, indicate a dowry to be assigned by the heir for the celebration of a certain number of Masses, there still remains a question whether the dowry was determined demonstratively or taxatively.

It is taxative if the testator designates first the dowry and then the number of Masses, *e. g.*, "*Lego ecclesiae fundum 'A' cum onere celebrandi quotannis decem Missas.*" In this case, the heir has no obligation of suppletion if the income decreases; a reduction of the Masses is to be sought. The dowry is determined demonstratively, if the testator should state first the obligation of Masses and then designate the dowry, *e. g.*, "*Haeres celebrare faciat quotannis decem Missas, pro quibus ipsi lego fundum;*" then the heir is bound to suppletion for the diminution of the income. Finally, if the testator commands the heir to give the ecclesiastical institute a certain dowry for Masses, the heir is bound by no obligation of suppletion.[57] St. Alphonsus[58] enumerates the causes for which the Apostolic See is accustomed to reduce Masses—lack of priests, slightness of the stipend or increase of the diocesan stipend, diminution of the income, or augmentation of the necessary expenses of life, or finally urgent necessity of those attached to the moral

---

[56] S. C. C., in Romana, 18 Apr. 1733; *apud Lucidi*, l.c., 29: "*De Vis. Sac. Lim.*," Cap. VII, 97; Benedict XIV.

[57] Gasparri, "*De Euch.*," I, 620; Benedict XIV, "*De Syn. Dioec.*," Lib. XIII, Cap. Ult., 32.

[58] "*Theol. Mor.*," Lib. VI, 331.

person bound by the foundation or of the fabric of the church or monastery.

Reduction is conceded for the internal forum by the Sacred Penitentiary; for the external forum by the Sacred Congregation of the Council; for missionary countries by the Sacred Congregation for the Propagation of the Faith; for faithful of the oriental rite, by the Sacred Congregation for the Oriental Church.[59] The reduction of founded Masses in churches of religious is granted by the S. C. pro Religiosis, as was noted at the end of the last chapter.[60]

Condonation has already been described as absolution given by competent authority for the omission of manual or founded Masses which should have been celebrated.

It is beyond controversy that condonation is reserved exclusively to the Roman Pontiff.[61] The Code does not change the old law. Gasparri says[62] that the legitimate Superior who can concede this absolution is the Roman Pontiff alone, who grants suppletion from the treasury of the Church, as Urban VIII and Innocent XII expressly stated.[63] Moreover, the Council of Trent presupposes that commutation of pious wills already accepted, as quasi-contracts, can be granted only by supreme ecclesiastical authority.[64] In one case only can the Bishop concede this absolution, when the founder conceded him this power.[65]

Condonation, as reduction, is conceded only for a just and proportionate cause. For founded Masses, the

---

59 Cappello, *"De Sac.,"* I, 720, 7.
60 Cfr. A. A. S., XI, 251.
61 Cappello, l.c., 721, 2.
62 *"De Euch.,"* I, 614.
63 Cfr. Innocent XII, const. *"Nuper,"* 23 dec. 1697; Fontes, 260.
64 Sess. XXII, de ref. c. 6.
65 Gasparri, *"De Euch.,"* I, 613.

income which remains must be insufficient for suppletion by the celebration of the omitted Masses.[66]

One who presumes to omit the celebration of Masses to which he is obliged, with malicious and unreasonable hope of absolution, is excluded from condonation. In this wise the Sacred Congregation of the Council has often issued decrees, which condemn such hope as unreasonable and illicit.[67]

Condonation is conceded when Masses have been inculpably omitted and sufficient income for the suppletion of the omissions is lacking.[68]

The Holy See, when it concedes condonation of omitted Masses, imposes a salutary penance, particularly the celebration of a certain number of Masses.[69]

In the index of faculties of Apostolic Delegates after the Code, one finds the following:

> "6. *Indulgendi ex causa paupertatis, iis qui Missarum sive manualium sive fundatarum applicationem omiserint, ut quod ad praeteritum tempus obligationem suam paulatim adimplere valeant, ita nempe, ut faciant quantum possunt pro integra satisfactione oneris Missarum quo gravantur, celebrando vel per se vel per alium singulis mensibus aliquem Missarum numerum, iuxta eorum vires, de bono et aequo a concedente et, in casibus occultis, a confessario determinandum.*
>
> *Moneantur autem praedictarum omissionum rei, si ita faciendo ante completam huiusmodi satisfactionem obierint, nec habeant quid pro eodem onere sive in toto sive in parte adimplendo relinquant,*

66 Cappello, "*De Sac.*," I, 721, 3.

67 Cappello, l.c.: Benedict XIV, "*De Syn. Dioec.*," Lib. XIII, Cap. Ult., 29; Lucidi, "*De Vis, Sac. Lim.*," Cap. VII, 80 sqq.; Gasparri, l. c., 614; Innocent XII, Const. "*Nuper*," 23 dec. 1697, Fontes, 260.

68 Gasparri, "*De Euch.*," I, 614, S. C. C. in Firmana, 21 Nov. 1761, Messan. 16 Maii, 1778, Anconitan, 20 Apr., 1782, Meleritan., 20 dec., 1788.

69 Gasparri, l.c., 615; Cappello, l.c., 721, 4.

Missas quae post eorum obitum celebrandae supererunt, ipsis, dum pie in Christo decedunt, condonatas fore censeri, defectum quemcumque tunc supplente Sancta Sede de thesauro Ecclesiae.

Item concedendi, si in aliquo casu ob peculiaria omnino rerum adiuncta expediens in Domino videatur, ut ad certum numerum iuxta vires petentis Missae, quod ad praeteritum pariter tempus, reducantur, dummodo non agatur de recidivis, supplente pariter Sanctitate Sua reliquarum Missarum defectum de Ecclesiae thesauro."

In such cases recourse to Rome may not be necessary. Appeal for a condonation should be made to the Apostolic Delegate.

Translation of Masses grants a commutation of the time or place determined for their celebration.[70]

Masses must be celebrated at the specified time. Whether anticipated or deferred application is invalid, or merely insufficient for the fulfillment of the obligation, or simply illicit, must be determined from the will of the founder. His will determines the obligation. If he wished celebration at that time and at no other, surely celebration at any other time would not fulfill the obligation contracted by the acceptance of the stipend. The obligation of Sunday Mass in a certain church for the convenience of the people, would presumably not be fulfilled by celebration on Saturday. The donor of the stipend seems not to have wished such a celebration. The obligation of restitution which binds when the obligation is not fulfilled, makes this a consideration of the gravest importance. The extent of such obligations is determined by the will of the donor of the stipend, evidenced or legitimately presumed.[71]

When the time of celebration is determined, transla-

[70] Gasparri, l.c., 621: Cappello, l.c., 722.
[71] Gasparri, l.c., 591.

tion is beyond episcopal power,[72] and recourse to the Apostolic See is necessary.[73] unless such power has been expressly conceded to the Bishop by the founder.

The transfer of Masses from the place determined for their celebration is within a Bishop's power if the founder has expressly granted him this power. Moreover, if a church can by no means be used for divine worship, and all ways of restoring it are closed, the obligations together with the income of that church, should be transferred by the local Ordinary to another church.[74] In these two cases, recourse to the Apostolic See is not required for the transfer of founded Masses.

The permission granted in canon 1187, had already been conceded by the Council of Trent.[75]

In other cases, transfers of place are reserved to the Apostolic See because such acts constitute a commutation

---

[72] S. R. C., in Neritonen., 17 Nov., 1657; *"Tuta conscientia nullatenus potuisse nec posse hujusmodi consuetudinem inducere et retinere."* The custom for the continuance of which permission had been requested, had already been allowed by the Bishop, that of celebrating anniversary Masses on Monday of each week, despite the specification of certain other days by the testators. Decr. Authen., 1040.

[73] Gasparri, l.c., 621.

[74] C. 1187; *"Si qua ecclesia nullo modo ad cultum divinum adhiberi possit et omnes aditus interclusi sint ad eam reficiendam, in usum profanum non sordidum ab Ordinario loci redigi potest, et onera cum reditibus titulusque paroeciae, si ecclesia sit paroecialis, in aliam ecclesiam ab eodem Ordinario transferantur."* Cappello, l.c., 722, 3.

[75] Sess. XXI, de ref., c. 7; " . . : *episcopi, etiam tanquam Apostolicae Sedis delegati, transferre possint beneficia simplicia, etiam juris patronatus, ex ecclesiis quae vetustate vel alias collapsae sint, et ob eorum inopiam nequeant instaurari, vocatis iis quorum interest, in matrices, aut alias ecclesias locorum eorumdem, seu viciniorum, arbitrio suo: atque in eisdem ecclesiis erigant altaria vel capellas sub eisdem invocationibus; vel in jam erecta altaria vel capellas transferant cum omnibus emolumentis et oneribus prioribus ecclesiis impositis."*

of pious wills, which is performed only by the supreme ecclesiastical authority.[76]

A just cause is always required for a translation of Masses. The Holy See concedes a transfer more easily if it is evident that the founder has desired only intercession for his soul, with little care for the place of celebration. For the sacrifice of the Mass is equally valuable for that end no matter where offered. When the founder appears to have been moved by a consideration of the place specified for the celebration of the Masses because of special devotion towards it or that the people might have Mass there, a transfer is gained with greater difficulty. The one and only cause for a transfer is that the Masses cannot be celebrated in that church or on that altar, because of a lack of priests.[77]

It is evident that the transfer of the onus of celebrating Masses implies the transfer of the goods.[78] The endowment was made to care for the necessary expenses of fulfilling the obligation, consequently a transfer of the total obligation involves a transfer of the dowry. If, however, some of the Masses can be celebrated on the proper altar or in the proper church, they should be there celebrated, especially on feast days. Then only a partial transfer takes place, the foundation is not transferred, but the stipends. The dowry is not to be transferred, but only the stipends for the Masses to be celebrated elsewhere.

The Ordinary should keep these things in mind when he applies an indult to transfer Masses. Gasparri[79] notes that since such indults were usually *"ad triennium,"* similarly his transfers should be temporary

[76] C. 1517, § 1: *"Ultimarum voluntatum reductio, moderatio, commutatio, quae fieri ex justa tantum et necessaria causa debent, Sedi Apostolicae reservantur, nisi fundator hanc potestatem etiam Ordinario loci expresse concesserit."*

[77] Gasparri l.c., 621.

[78] Gasparri, l.c., 621; Cappello, l.c., 722, 4.

[79] L.c., 621.

whenever possible. This was prescribed in the formula of the indult. After the Code, such indults are usually "*ad quinquennium*" and it is expressly said in the formula that the transfers should be similarly "*ad quinquennium.*"[80]

Closely allied to the transfer of foundations is the transfer by virtue of law or Apostolic indult, of founded stipends which cannot be applied in the proper place or by the proper priests according to the specifications of the foundation. Such transferred stipends are termed "*ad instar manualium.*"[81]

He who has a number of Masses of which he may freely dispose, may distribute them among priests of his choice, provided he knows they are absolutely trustworthy or are recommended by the testimony of their Ordinary.[82]

A distinction between the transfer of manual, "*ad instar manualium*" and founded stipends is not expressly contained in this canon. That such is its meaning, however, was proven by a decree of the Sacred Congregation of the Council on the 19th of Feb., 1921.[83]

The Congregation was asked whether the Code, and in particular canon 838, abrogated, according to canon 6, §1, the Conciliar law of the ecclesiastical province to which it pertained, in which the following was decreed: "*Nominatim prohibemus Missas celebrandas dare extra uniuscujusque dioecesis ambitum absque Ordinarii permissione.*" Some held, so said the Ordinary who petitioned the response, this Conciliar law to be "*praeter,*" not "*contra*" canon 838, while others rejected this view and embraced the opposite opinion.

80 Cfr. Vermeersch, "*Epit. Juris Canonici,*" II, 871, III.
81 C. 826, § 2.
82 C. 838; "*Qui habent Missarum numerum de quibus sibi liceat libere disponere, possunt eas tribuere sacerdotibus sibi acceptis, dummodo probe sibi constet eos esse omni exceptione maiores vel testimonio proprii Ordinarii commendatos.*"
83 A. A. S., XIII, 228.

The response of the Congregation to the doubt whether and how the disposition of that Provincial Council is sustained in the case, was: *"Quoad Missas fundatas, vel ad instar manualium, vel manuales datas intuitu causae piae, affirmative: in reliquis servetur* can. 838 *Codicis Iuris Canonici."*

By common law, then, the Ordinary can forbid the transfer of founded and *"ad instar manualium"* stipends outside his diocese. Unless he does so, these stipends are transferred freely according to canon 838.

The *"animadversiones"* according to which the above response was given, state the reasons for the decision. Note that these considerations are in reference to a general disposition of law by which the condition of permission of one's Ordinary is exacted for the transfer of stipends outside the diocese. Such a disposition *"non tantum juri Codicis sed etiam iuri Superiori, ut decretis S. Congregationis initio hujus saeculi est sancitum, contradicere, simulque non solum praeter sed vere contra canones esse, demonstratur. Sed praetereunda non est specialis auctoritas quam in certa stipendia possidet Episcopus exjurisdictione et alta administratione quae ei competit respectu multarum ecclesiarum et locorum piorum. Stipendia enim dari vel legari possunt tum personis tum locis. In priori casu, sacerdos libere utetur iure sibi concesso can.* 838. *In altero casu, rector ecclesiae vel loci pii subjecti Ordinario loci normas ab Ordinario praescriptas in transmittendis stipendiis quae exuberant observare debebit."*

Must the whole stipend always be transferred or is it sometimes legitimate to retain a part because of an extrinsic title?

When *"ad instar manualium"* stipends are transferred, one may, unless the mind of the founder forbid, remit only the manual stipend of the diocese in which the Mass is celebrated and legitimately retain the excess, if the generous stipend holds the place of part of the dowry of a benefice or pious cause.[84]

Vermeersch[85] gives a reason for this legislation. The founder has not only prescribed Masses, but also help for a certain church: accordingly he is considered to have desired to benefit those who profit by a foundation in that church. The Code, however, does not absolutely permit the retention of part of a generous stipend for a founded Mass as often as those Masses are celebrated elsewhere or by a different priest than the founder specified, but places this condition—if the greater stipend constitutes a partial dowry of the benefice or pious cause. The will of the founder is here, as always, the rule for the transfer of the stipend. This is doubly clear from the general exception expressed in the early part of the canon; "*nisi obstet mens fundatoris.*" If it is clear that the founder wishes all the stipend to go to the celebrant of the Mass, the stipend must always be transferred in full.

"Each and every administrator of pious institutions or anyone else who is obliged to attend to the saying of holy Masses for stipends, whether clerics or laymen, must at the end of each year, send to their Ordinaries, those stipends for which they have not yet satisfied, according to the manner to be specified by the Ordinary."[86]

Secular priests and lay people, and also religious, unless they pertain to an exempt clerical religious insti-

---

84 C. 840, § 2; "*In Missis ad instar manualium, nisi obstet mens fundatoris, legitime retinetur excessus et satis est remittere solam elleemosynam manualem dioecesis in qua Missa celebratur, si pinguis eleemosyna locum pro parte teneat dotis beneficii aut causae piae.*"

85 "Epit. Iur. Can.," II, 107, 4.

86 Woywod, "The New Canon Law," 684; c. 841, § 1: "*Omnes et singuli administratores causarum piarum aut quoquo modo ad Missarum onera implenda obligati, sive ecclesiastici sive laici, sub exitum cuiuslibet anni, Missarum onera quibus nondum fuerit satisfactum, suis Ordinariis tradant secundum modum ab his definiendum.*"

tute, when their Ordinary is their Major Superior, must send these stipends to the local Ordinary.[87]

The phrase *"sub exitum cuiuslibet anni"* is not to be accepted mathematically, but morally. If anyone, at the end of the year, has Masses for the celebration of which two or three months still remain according to the will of the donor, he is not held to send them to his Ordinary. *A fortiori,* if the will of the donor is that the Masses be celebrated in a certain church or on a certain altar, a priest may retain some Masses at the end of the year lest he be without stipends.[88]

The year is to be understood in such wise that for stipends *"ad instar manualium"* the obligation of sending them to the Ordinary begins at the end of the year during which they should have been celebrated; for manual stipends, one year from the day on which they were accepted, saving the different will of the donors.[89]

For *"ad instar manualium"* stipends, the year is to be taken civilly, so that such Masses are remitted to the Ordinary at the end of December of that year during which they should have been celebrated.[90]

The right and duty to see that the obligations of Masses are fulfilled in secular churches, belong to the local Ordinary; in churches of religious, to their Superiors.[91]

This canon regulates vigilance over the fulfillment of both manual and founded Masses.[92] The Superiors of non-exempt religious institutes, then, have the right and

---

87 Cfr. c. 198, § 1.

88 Cappello, l.c., 712.

89 C. 841, § 2; *"Hoc autem tempus ita est accipiendum ut in Missis ad instar manualium obligatio eas deponendi decurrat a fine illius anni intra quem onera impleri debuissent; in manualibus vero, post annum a die suscepti oneris, salva diversa offerentium voluntate."*

90 Cappello, l.c., 712.

91 C. 842; *"Ius et officium advigilandi ut onera Missarum ad impleantur, in ecclesiis saecularium pertinet ad loci Ordinarium; in religiosorum ecclesiis, ad eorum Superi ores."*

92 Cappello, l.c., 713, 2.

duty of vigilance over the celebration of founded Masses in their churches. The same Superiors are bound by the obligation of inspecting either personally or by delegates, the books in which Masses are noted.[93]

At the same time, vigilance over the execution of obligations of founded Masses in churches of non-exempt religious pertains to the local Ordinary.[94]

Vigilance over the fulfillment of founded Masses in churches of non-exempt religious pertains by canon 842 to the religious Superiors, by canon 1515 and 1550 to the local Ordinary. Since the vigilance of the local Ordinary is not explicitly exclusive, it may be that the fulfillment of founded Masses in this case is under the vigilance of the religious Superior and also under the vigilance of the local Ordinary. Or it may be that the Code grants vigilance over only manual Masses to the Superiors of non-exempt religious, since canon 842 is more generic in its object than canon 1515 and 1550. These canons, specifically for pious wills, including founded Masses, may be powerful enough to exclude founded Masses from canon 842. In either case, the fulfillment of founded Masses is subject finally to the vigilance of the local Ordinary, whether or not a share in this vigilance is conceded to the religious Superior when the foundation is in a church of non-exempt religious.

---

93 Fanfani, "*De Iure Religiosorum*," 388, C; c. 843, § 1; "*Rectores ecclesiarum aliorumque piorum locorum sive saecularium sive religiosorum in quibus eleemosynae Missarum recipi solent, peculiarem habeant librum in quo accurate notent Missarum receptarum numerum, intentionem, eleemosynam, celebrationem.*

§ 2. *Ordinarii tenentur obligatione singulis saltem annis huiusmodi libros sive per se ipsi sive per alios recognoscendi.*"

94 Fanfani, "*De Iure Religiosorum*," 174, A; Cfr. cc. 1550, 1515, § 2.

BIBLIOGRAPHY

Sources

Acta Apostolicae Sedis, Romae, 1909sqq.
Amplissima Collectio Conciliorum, Mansi, Parisiis, 1903.
Canones et Decreta Concilii Tridentini, Taurini, 1913.
Codex Iuris Canonici, Romae, 1918.
Codicis Iuris Canonici Fontes, Gasparri, Romae, 1923.
Collectanea Sacra Congregationis de Propaganda Fide, Romae, 1907.
Corpus Iuris Canonici, Lipsiae, 1922.
Corpus Iuris Civilis Romani, Coloniae Munatianae, 1718.
Decreta Authentica Congregationis Sacrorum Rituum, Romae, 1901.

References

S. Alphonsus, Mariae de Liguori, Theologia Moralis, Ratisbonae, 1880.
Augustine, Charles, A Commentary on Canon Law, St. Louis, 1921.
Ayrinhac, H., General Legislation in the New Code of Canon Law, New York, 1923.
Bargilliat, M., Praelectiones Juris Canonici, Parisiis, 1923.
Berlendi, Francesco, Delle Obblazioni All' Altare Antiche e Moderne, Venetiis, 1736.
Benedict XIV, De Sanctissimo Missae Sacrificio, Prati, 1843.
Benedict XIV, De Synodo Dioecesana, Romae, 1806.
Binterim, Die Vorzuglichsten Denkwurdigkeiten der Christ-Katholischen Kirche, 7 vols. in 17, Mainz, 1828.
Blat, Albert, Commentarium Textus Codicis Juris Canonici, Romae, 1920.

Cappello, Felix, Tractatus Canonico-Moralis de Sacramentis, Taurinorum Augustae, 1921.
Catholic Encyclopedia, The, New York, 1913.
Cocchi, Guidus, Commentarium in Codicem Iuris Canonici, Romae, 1924.
De Giudice, Vincenzo, Stipendia Missarum, Romae, 1922.
Denzinger, Henrico, Enchiridion Symbolorum et Definitionum, St. Louis, 1921.
Fanfani, P. Louis, De Iure Religiosorum, Romae, 1925.
Ferreres, Juan, Las Misas Manuales, Madrid, 1924.
Gennari, Casimir, Consultazioni Morali-Canoniche-Liturgiche, Romae, 1904.
Gasparri, Tractatus Canonicus de Sanctissima Eucharistia, Parisiis, 1897.
Godfrey, John, The Right of Patronage according to the Code of Canon Law, Washington, 1924.
Keller, Charles, Mass Stipends, Washington, 1925.
Lucidi, De Visitatione Sacrorum Liminum, Romae, 1883.
Maroto, Philippo, Institutiones Iuris Canonici, Romae, 1921.
Pallottini, Collectio Omnium Conclusionum et Resolutionum Sacrae Congregationis Concilii, Romae, 1887.
Pasqualigo, Zachariae, De Sacrificio Novae Legis Quaestiones Theologicae, Morales, Juridicae, Venetiis, 1707.
Pignatelli, Consultationes Canonicae, Coloniae Allobrogum, 1700.
Schmalzgrueber, Francisco, Jus Ecclesiasticum Universum, Romae, 1844.
Tamburini, Thomas, Opera Omnia, Venetiis, 1702.
Thomassinus, Ludovicus, Vetus et Nova Ecclesiae Disciplina circa Beneficia et Beneficiarios, Magontiaci, 1787.
Vermeersch, A., Epitome Iuris Canonici, Romae, 1922.
Wernz, Francisco, Jus Decretalium, Romae, 1901.
Woywod, Stanislaus, The New Canon Law, New York, 1918.

Facultas Canonica

Universitas Catholica Americae

Washingtonii

1926

No. 34

DEUS LUX MEA

THESES

QUAS

AD DOCTORATUS GRADUM

IN

JURE CANONICO

Apud Universitatem Catholicam Americae

CONSEQUENDUM

PUBLICE PROPUGNABIT

NEWTON THOMAS MILLER

SACERDOS ARCHIDIOECESIS

PHILADELPHIENSIS

IURIS CANONICI LICENTIATUS

HORA XI A. M. DIE XXVIII MAII A. D. MCMXXVI
JUS CANONICUM

ROMAN LAW

XLV. Modification, Suspension and Extinction of Personality
XLVI. Cura and Tutela
XLVII. Moral Persons

THE INSTITUTES OF GAIUS

XLVIII. Liberty and Slavery
XLIX. Citizenship
L. The Roman Family

INTERNATIONAL LAW

LI. The Notion of International Law
LII. Fundamental Principles and Sources
LIII. General Rights and Duties of States
LIV. Self-Preservation and Intervention
LV. Immunity
LVI. Consuls
LVII. Extradition
LVIII. Piracy
LIX. The Drago Doctrine
LX. The Monroe Doctrine

* * * * * *

VIDIT FACULTAS:

PHILIPPUS BERNARDINI, S. T. D., J. U. D., Decanus.

H. LUDOVICUS MOTRY, S. T. D., J. C. D., a Secretis.

VIDIT RECTOR UNIVERSITATIS:

†THOMAS J. SHAHAN, S. T. D., J. U. L.

BIOGRAPHY

Newton Thomas Miller was born on November 12, 1899, at Philadelphia, Pennsylvania. His primary education was received at St. Stephen's Parochial School. After pursuing high school studies at St. Stephen's School and La Salle College, he entered the Seminary of St. Charles Borromeo, Overbrook, in the fall of 1915. On May 29th, 1924, he was ordained to the priesthood by His Eminence D. Cardinal Dougherty.

In the fall of the same year he enrolled in the School of Canon Law of the Catholic University of America at Washington. His grateful appreciation is extended to his professors for their generous and kind assistance.

www.ingramcontent.com/pod-product-compliance
Lightning Source LLC
LaVergne TN
LVHW050157080826
844660LV00012B/310

* 9 7 8 0 8 1 3 2 2 2 2 4 0 *